Great words about *Messy* ‹

"If you want to get rid of the clutter in your life and learn how to keep what's good and let go of what weighs you down, read this book. In *Messy to Meaningful,* the authors will have you laughing out loud as you discover how to make positive changes, apply biblical truth, release the unnecessary, and get personally and spiritually organized. You can read this book on your own, but I highly recommend going through it with a group of friends as you learn to live in a new kind of freedom."

~**Carol Kent, Speaker and Author**
He Holds My Hand: Experiencing God's
Presence & Protection **(Tyndale)**

"*Messy to Meaningful* will lead you to sort through your life to discover not only the gold nuggets you've been looking for, but an occasional chocolate bar."

~**Linda Evans Shepherd, Author**
Winning Your Daily Spiritual Battles

"As a junk junkie, I found this book enormously helpful. While reading the chapter on pens, I did a lead count and discovered 38 writing utensils in one drawer. And I have four junk drawers. Sigh. *Messy to Meaningful's* message rings true, that stuff that we stuff—not just physically, but spiritually too—needs to be periodically sorted and discarded. 'Out of sight, out of mind' doesn't work with junk. It never goes away. It just keeps accumulating, cluttering, and adding unnecessary stress. The good stuff gets harder and harder to dig out beneath it. That's why I adore this book so much; it gives me tools and motivation to tackle the junk in my life, both physical and spiritual. Yep. Decluttering empowers and frees us. And makes sure our blessings outweigh our stressings."

~**Debora M. Coty, award-winning author of**
more than 40 books, including the bestselling
***Too Blessed to be Stressed* series**

"How can emptying a junk drawer get rid of so much junk in 'real' life? Rhonda, Monica, and Kaley have taken that messy, common space in everyone's home—that space you hope no one looks in—and have used it as a brilliant and biblical word picture of how to get whole and healthy—and they've done it with a dash of humor. If you want to get rid of the stuff that holds you down so God can lift you up, this book is for you. *Messy to Meaningful* is one book you will never find in a junk drawer!"

~Pam Farrel, bestselling author of 45 books including *Discovering Hope in the Psalms: A Creative Bible Study Experience; 7 Simple Skills for Every Woman: Success In Keeping It All Together;* and *Men Are Like Waffles, Women Are Like Spaghetti*

"I've looked into the junk drawer in my kitchen countless times. I never discovered God-moments there, but my friends, Rhonda Rhea, Kaley Rhea, and Monica Schmelter have done exactly that in their book, *Messy to Meaningful: Lessons from the Junk Drawer.* With great insight flavored by their delightful personalities, they discuss the junk in our lives that deters us from serving God, what we can do about it, and the precious spiritual lessons we can discover in those moments. I love this book!"

~Michelle Cox, author of *When God Calls the Heart: Devotions from Hope Valley* (www. WhenGodCallstheHeart.com) and *Just 18 Summers* (www.just18summers.com)

Lessons from the Junk Drawer

Monica Schmelter, Rhonda Rhea, and Kaley Rhea

Bold Vision Books
PO Box 2011
Friendswood, Texas 77549

Copyright © 2018, Monica Schmelter, Rhonda Rhea, Kaley Rhea
ISBN9781-946708-229
Library of Congress Control Number: 2018940242
Cover Art by © Matthew Kay | Dreamstime.com
Cover Design by Maddie Scott
Interior Design by Maddie Scott and Karen Porter
Published in the United States of America.
Bold Vision Books, PO Box 2011, Friendswood, Texas 77549
* Most names changed to protect privacy and redemption.

dedication

To our mentor, colleague, coach, and dear friend,

Karen Porter.

Thank you for pouring into the lives of so many for the sake of the Kingdom. How blessed we are to be three of those lives.

table of contents

acknowledgments

Monica

Much love and big hugs to my husband Joe. Your encouragement and support mean so much to me. I still remember the day we met. I had been working at the racquetball club for a whopping 5 minutes when you walked in with your dad and sister. When the person training me said this is the Schmelter family and you'll be seeing a lot of them, I laughed. Who knew I'd be seeing you for the rest of my life? I love you Joe, and I am thankful for the life we share. To my one and only son also named Joe I love you BIG. I appreciate your help in fixing all of my devices. Whether it's my cell phone, laptop, desktop or some other gadget you are always willing (at least mostly willing) to help me. Thank you for your love and support. Many times I joke about being *Monica in the Middle* of my two Joe's but I wouldn't have it any other way. To both of you I tip my hat and say "We're going to make it after all."

Here's a big shout out to Herman and Sharron Bailey. You've both been examples, leaders, mentors, and friends to me for years. Your consistency, integrity, and encouragement have meant so much. Herman, I know I can always text you and that you'll be honest and encouraging. You have both helped me through writing this book and I appreciate it so much. There is not enough time to name everyone—but I am one grateful woman. I am blessed to have so many trustworthy friends. I am grateful for God's love. I am thankful He rescued me and continues to lead me through life's journeys. Jesus you have been my constant. At my worst and best moments you have been faithful. I bask in your love and trust you to perfect everything that concerns me.

Rhonda

As always, huge thanks, hugs and kisses to my hubby and hero, Richie Rhea. Your love, encouragement, teaching, discipleship, and leadership are book fuel for sure—life fuel, even. You are my favorite human of all time.

Thank yous all around for the rest of my fam. I love you so Andy, Amber, Asa, and Amos Rhea, Jordan Rhea, writer-bud, Kaley Rhea, Allie, Derek, Emerson and Oswyn McMullin, Daniel, Olivia and Ainsley Rhea. You are the best pray-ers/supporters/encouragers!

Heartfelt gratitude to George Porter, Karen Porter, Maddie Scott, Karen Dockrey, and all the talented and beautifully ministry-minded folks at Bold Vision Books who've had a creative hand in this project.

I'm so thankful for my agent and friend, Pamela Harty, who shares my heart for ministry, and thankful, too, for the helpful people at The Knight Agency who help make it possible for me to do what I love to do.

Christianne Rhoads and Rhoads Graphics, you are a delight and a blessing. Thank you for your web and branding design and your wonderful ministry support and counsel. And most of all, your friendship!

Additional thank yous to my good friends and fellow laborers at LifeWay's *HomeLife* magazine, Right to the Heart's *Leading Hearts* magazine, Missouri Baptist Convention's *The Pathway*, Munce's *More to Life*, Edie Melson's *Write Conversation*, *Blue Ridge Mountains Christian Writers*, and the many other publications who generously give me column space for all kinds of nonsense—and for kindly supporting me in re-sharing some of that nonsense in this book.

Special thanks to AWSA, the Advanced Writers and Speakers Association, my heart-sisters who share support, knowledge, godly insights and powerful prayers.

More nods of thanks to my church family at Troy First Baptist Church for consistent prayers and encouragement. You're the sweetest.

My amazing prayer team—wonderful warrior women! My sincere gratitude to you all for keeping this project bathed in prayer: Janet Bridgeforth, Tina Byus, Diane Campbell, Mary Clark, Theresa Easterday, Chris Hendrickson, Melinda Massey, and Peanuts Rudolph. Oh how I cherish these women!

Monica Schmelter, I fully believe your idea for this book was straight from the Father. How grateful I am that you, and He, let me come along for this adventure. And to have Kaley Rhea here too? Just that much fuller of the funs and the adventures. Thank you, co-author buddies!

My deepest gratitude is ever reserved to the One who saved me by His amazing grace, miraculously redeeming my mess, and then sent me on the most grand adventure of faith. To my Lord and Savior, Jesus Christ,

Thank You for Your constant presence, for Your grace, Your mercy, Your empowering and Your indescribable love. You ARE the meaning.

Kaley

Many many thanks to my Missouri Baptist University fam—Dr. Sheri Brandt, Edie Beamer, and Donna Krone—for putting up with my hectic writing schedule and for being so flexible and supportive throughout the ups and downs of crafting this book. You make my day job a day joy.

Shout out to my good buddy, Rachel Hilderbrand, for being an awesome friend in general and for teaching me by example how to be a healthy communicator in particular. Also, I would like to acknowledge your cool baby son. I'm talking about you, Eli. (He knows.)

To my sibs who are the greatest sibs. Andrew Rhea, Amber Rhea, Jordan Rhea, Allie McMullin, Derek McMullin, Daniel Rhea, and Olivia Rhea. You are the most fun people, and I'm absurdly proud of you. I just want to share meals with you and beat you at sports forever. That is all.

And you know I have to say a word about my papa, Richie Rhea, whose support, encouragement, wisdom, quirks, example, and love mean the world to me. Everyone should get to have a dad like you.

I'm beyond grateful for and awestruck by my co-authors. Mommy and Monica; you two are ridiculous. So wise and hilarious and kind and kinda crazy. Thank you, thank you, thank you for including me. This journey's already been full of fruit and special blessings, and I would've been happy just hanging out with you two, but we actually get to *work together*! I want to tell everyone we're friends. Everyone, look at my cool friends! We work together, and we're besties! Love your insights and your hearts and your unique you-nesses.

And to my Savior. My life. My joy. My friend. My meaning.

You're so good. You are goodness. I want all my days to be full of love notes to You.

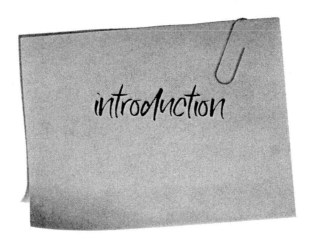

Can't Close the Drawer? First, Empty It

Everyone has one, right? The junk drawer. Oh, the stuff we stuff. We stuff it right in there. Stuff it all willy-nilly-like until we can't even close it. Super glue that is no longer super—or glue. Ponytail holders from ponytails we can't pony up anymore. Candies that long ago lost their wrappers. Packets of seeds we'll never plant. It's almost sad. It's like an assemblage of strays:

> Stray tools, stray clips,
> Stray goops, stray pics,
> Stray earphones for days,
> Stray glitters, stray sprays.
> Even stray glitter-sprays.

Have you ever found glitter spray in your junk drawer so old it will neither glitter nor spray?

Most of us have stuffed pieces of our past in that drawer. Items we can't seem to let go of—some we hold onto for absolutely no good reason—and items we think we might need later. The funny thing is, you hardly ever plan a junk drawer. Want it or not, that junk collection is happening.

The collection happens in our lives too. As a matter of fact, we can hold on to so much junk that it becomes tough to fit in the good things the Lord is calling us to. Do you recognize in yourself any of these signs you may need to sort some of your junk?

* Life seems so full you're not sure you can handle it.
* You're upset—and you don't quite know why.
* The tiniest obstacle can freak you out or set you off.
* You're surprised by the fear you're experiencing.
* You feel like an utter failure—practically all the time.
* Contentment seems to always belong to someone else, not you.
* Peace appears to be always just out of reach.

Sometimes we stuff stray items into our lives without thinking. Other times we hold on to incidentals we simply no longer need. **But what if we told you there are ways to sort through some of that junk, keep what you need, throw out what's unnecessary and move forward, less hindered, less weighted down, more spiritually organized—more...*free?***
The truth is, we have an amazing God who can take our craziest messes and bring about glorious beauty and purpose.

Messy to Meaningful

We are three of the messiest. We met on the set of *The Bridges* TV show (Monica was interviewing Rhonda and Kaley), and it wasn't long at all before we knew we shared a heart for the message of this book. Each of us can tell stories of God's redemption through so much messy. Each of us, by the way, can also testify that we have messes yet to sort, and that we rely daily on the grace of God for the mess-ups we'll likely experience in the future. His Word is our truth-source, and His grace is so much bigger than any mess. Any of our messes. Or any of yours.
God's grace and His redemptive power is evident even in the way He brought the three of us together to write this

book—three such different people, from such different perspectives, in such different writing styles. When three people with such different personalities write a book together, wouldn't you expect to find things stuffed in the book rather willy-nilly like the junkiest junkety-junk drawer?

Seriously. How messy should this be? Yet we have watched as the Lord has graciously brought us together in heart—and brought this book together as well—with great agreement borne of love for Him and with love for each other, completely united in purpose. In the end, His grace wrought the deepest and most marvelous meaning! And while your average junk drawer is not planned by its creator, we have no doubt that this book-about-junk was planned by our infinitely creative Creator. We have come out the other side of this book's writing closer than ever, and with a shared excitement about how our God might want to use the book. Closer to each other. Closer to Him. *Thank You, Father.*

We're also amazed and delighted about how we've enjoyed each other's different styles, how we've learned from each other, and how we've learned so much from sharing His Word together. We're praying that will happen for you, our readers, also. There is such power in God's Word!

We've included extra thoughts, questions, and passages for further reflection at the end of each chapter in the "Sorting It Out" section. In some chapters you'll find a brief charge or two. Then some chapters provide weightier thoughts, longer assignments, and points to ponder. Other chapters land somewhere in between. We're hoping there will be something for everyone. We encourage you to sort through the sorting questions and focus most on the ones that are the best fit for you, giving the others lighter attention when you need to.

Our desire is that He will use this book in your life personally, friends, as He has in ours. These are our prayers for you:

From Monica

Dear God, I thank You that You are not deterred by our messes. You are the friend who sticks closer than a brother, and I thank You for Your promise to never leave or forsake us. Please work in the heart of each reader to bring meaning and beauty. Where our faith needs to be stretched, give us grace. In places we are tempted to settle for the quick fix, give us the strength and patience to wait on You by faith. As we sort through the junk drawers of our lives, light our hearts on fire with Your unconditional love. You are the potter and we are the clay, so we trust You to bring meaning and true beauty in our lives. We pray all this in the matchless Name of Jesus Christ. Amen.

From Rhonda

Heavenly Father, I ask that You would even now be readying the heart of each of our reader-friends. If there are pieces of the past any one of those friends is holding onto, I pray You will inspire and empower the process of letting go. Empty us of us, fill us with You. Those places where we need to hold more tightly to You, I ask that You will give the desire and the ability to do that, as well. I ask that You will, by Your Holy Spirit, work in the hearts of each person who picks up this book, confronting, convicting, convincing of truth—cleaning out any junk that isn't needed and ultimately, by Your grace, bringing Your grand and glorious meaning from every single mess. All by Your power and in the name of Jesus, Amen.

From Kaley

Dear Heavenly Father, how easily we are overwhelmed. As we journey through this book and through these lives You've gifted us to live, help us to be utterly overwhelmed by You. By Your beauty. Your mercy. Your love. And let us see the earthly things we thought were so overwhelming—the messes and the trials and the mounds of malcontent—for what they are. The finite never seems as overwhelming held up against the overwhelming infinite. Give us joy as You have joy. Help us grieve the way You grieve. Fashion boundaries of Your wisdom around destructive patterns of thinking, and remove any boundaries we've built around ourselves out of fear. Your works are wonderful, Lord, and we know it. Full well. Let us smile at the thought of You; move us to tears with affection for You. Lord, I am not here to ugly cry at a Hallmark commercial and then be unmoved listening to the Words of my sweet Savior. I'm here for You. We're here for You. Bringing our mess before You as an offering. Whatever You'd like to do, Lord, here we are.

chapter 1

Rubber Bands: Stretching Your Faith

Monica Schmelter

Then he said to the man, "Stretch out your hand." And the man stretched it out, and it was restored, healthy like the other.
(Matthew 12:13)

Most people have at least one junk drawer. I'm a classic overachiever: I have one in my kitchen and I also have one in my office at work. The one in my office contains a collection of vital items I've accumulated over the years.

The stuff in my office could easily be mistaken for junk. But since I know each item's backstory, I'm more keenly aware of lessons that can be found in the junk drawer. Take for instance the very long but busted rubber bands I tied together and placed in my office junk drawer. The busted rubber bands appear worthless.

The rubber bands, however, once served a great purpose. They were used as part of an object lesson that we at our Christian television station referred to as the Blessed-are-those-who- stretch-their-faith-for-they-shall-overcome-obstacles lessons. Those stretched-out rubber bands were on display at several staff meetings and then proudly taped to my office door. That reminder gave us a lot of laughs and amens. They helped moved our team forward. As a ministry team, we were challenged with obstacles daily. A big one was our rented facility with the leak. It wasn't just a small leak either. Whenever it rained outside, it rained inside. At one point our office and studio flooded so frequently that we placed our computer towers on plastic containers. We did the same with electrical cords. It was hard work and sometimes the whole office and studio reeked because of the dampness.

While my team was energetic and committed, life and ministry were disrupted each time we were forced to grab the ShopVac® or cancel studio productions at a moment's notice due to rain. It was exhausting trying to keep our building even usable. Our landlord proved unhelpful so our team pulled together, prayed, cleaned, and applied the rubber band lesson to stretching our faith.

Stretched to the Limit

After weeks of obstacles and relentless stretching, one team member grew tired and despondent. She stood up in our team meeting and said she was nearing the breaking point. The tears poured. The room grew uncomfortably quiet. Those rubber bands that were taped to my office door as an encouragement were becoming a reminder instead of what it's like to be stretched and broken—maybe beyond repair.

I wondered what I should do. This whole stretch thing had started out with the best of intentions. But this group of people I love dearly had at least one team member (I figured there were more, but she was the only one brave enough to speak up.) at the breaking point.

Now I may be an overachiever when it comes to junk drawers, but I wasn't immediately sure how to respond to the tears and silence. I didn't know what to say next. I stammered, stuttered, and then circled our group around our hurting teammate and prayed blessing and strength for her. I asked God for His help and direction. I asked Him to help us know how much to stretch and how to obey Him in the midst of the breaking point.

After that meeting ended, I continued to seek God and ask for His help and perspective in the whole situation. He is so gracious and patient. He began to show me that there are many times that He asks us to stretch. The man with the withered hand was one of the first examples that came to my mind (Matt. 12:10-13).

In Front of Everybody?

How often have I read that passage and thought about how hard it must have been for that man to stretch forth his withered hand in front of an angry congregation? God took the one thing that had caused this man embarrassment and shame—that withered hand—and asked him to stretch it out in front of everybody.

The moment the man obeyed, Jesus healed him immediately. It involved stretching and obedience. It involved being uncomfortable. It involved a congregation who had no idea what was happening. It included religious leaders who had no interest in healing on this particular day. These leaders were angry about the healing and hostility filled the room. Yet the healing happened. In the man's stretch, his healing came.

The man probably felt stretched beyond his breaking point. Just like the young woman I worked with. Stretching comes complete with discomfort. Yet when stretching is an obedience to God's Word, stretching is richly rewarded.

That team meeting included stretching, crying, praying, bravery, and honesty. The young woman's honesty brought us to a new place as a team. Her willingness to share her fears and pain led us to come up with new ideas and to more emphatically believe God when all looks dark. This brought growth and togetherness to our entire group. Maybe not right away, but it happened.

Surrender to the Stretch

As a whole team, we updated the rubber band object lesson display. After all, we had all learned the valuable lesson that when we are stretched beyond our breaking point God is up to something good. When we trust God in the stretch, we begin to grow and bear fruit as never before. We began to pray for one another more often and began to operate in an even greater level of love and unity. We also laughed more often.

One very rainy Tuesday, our rented facility also lost power. There was a torrential downpour outside and a flood inside. Since the electricity was out we couldn't start the ShopVac®. We lit candles. Our station was off the air, and there was nothing we could do about it. In the midst of this stretching day, the same young woman who had burst into tears some weeks before began to belt out "It Is Well with My Soul." And she meant it. The team joined in singing. We raised our hands, in surrender to the stretch. We trusted God.

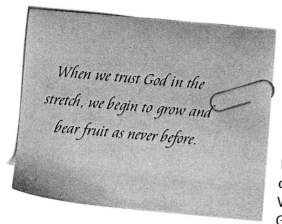

When we trust God in the stretch, we begin to grow and bear fruit as never before.

I'd love to tell you that the rain stopped but it didn't. It went on for days. Thankfully, the electricity was restored after a few hours, and we got our station back on the air. Rain was still soaking our office and studio. What to do? We praised God and did what we could in the stretch.

It's been 15 years since we huddled together singing "It is Well with my Soul." Since that time, we packed up and moved into a new studio and office building. Our new facility doesn't leak and we're not renters anymore. Now, we only grab the ShopVac® when we're building new sets in the studio.

We all face situations that stretch us. In those situations, we can stretch out what brings us pain and give it to Christ. The healing may be instantaneous. I love it when that happens. Or it may happen through a process. But as we stretch, He sees and answers. When we're stretched beyond our limits, we can be sure God is up to something good.

Sorting It Out

Let's look at Matthew 12:10-13: "And a man was there with a withered hand. And they asked him, 'Is it lawful to heal on the Sabbath?'—so that they might accuse him. He said to them, 'Which one of you who has a sheep, if it falls into a pit on the Sabbath, will not take hold of it and lift it out? Of how much more value is a man than a sheep! So it is lawful to do good on the Sabbath. Then he said to the man, 'Stretch out your hand.' And the man stretched it out, and it was restored, healthy like the other."

One of the things we see is the heart of Jesus is to be good to His children. He sees our withered places and does not turn away in disgust. He challenges us to trust Him with our withered places and sometimes in the midst of people who may not understand. We see this man is obedient to Christ in the midst of all kinds of stuff that is out of his control.

List some of the specific areas in your life where you are being stretched.

_____

_____

_____

Pray over each of these stretches and commit them to God by asking Him for the help, courage, and healing that you need. write your prayer here.

_____

_____

_____

What is God teaching you in the stretch?

_____

_____

_____

What good is coming during each of the stretches?

_____

_____

_____

Ask the Lord to continue to give you the courage to stretch in faith before Him. Ask Him for His wisdom and perspective in what He's doing in your life despite the painful stretches. In particularly challenging times it can be helpful to remind yourself that, whatever God is doing in your life, He is going to bring you good. You may want to write this verse out and carry it in your wallet to help you in most stretching moments:

"For I know the plans I have for you, declares
the LORD, plans for welfare and not for evil, to
give you a future and a hope"
(Jeremiah 29:11).

Staples: Staple-Seeking and the Staple of Seeking

Rhonda Rhea

*Seek the LORD and his strength; seek his
presence continually!*
(Psalm 105:4)

Nobody knows the staples I've seen. In my last trip through the junk drawer, oh man. I found staples. And then more staples. Then some giant staples. Then tiny little baby staples. What could those baby ones possibly do? Attach tiny-baby papers to other tiny-baby papers?

The weird part was not so much the number of staples, though there were approximately 80 billion. The weird part wasn't even the fact that there were so many sizes, shapes and colors, though it was an 80-billion-part rainbow assortment. No, the weird part was that I found no stapler. Not one. I searched diligently for one—any size, any shape, any color. And then I searched again. Because it didn't make sense that I would have ten tons of stapler-less staples. What was I even supposed to do with all those homeless, jobless staples?

Search High and Low—Without the Low

I wish I could tell you that only happens in my junk drawer. Or that it's only about staples. But I just finished digging through my purse for about 20 minutes, desperately searching for a business card that I'd stuck in there a few days ago. Know what I found instead? Yeah, besides the candy bar of unknown origin. Or age. I found instead the list I spent 20 minutes searching for yesterday. I have proven once again that it's not just about the looking. It's also about the overlooking. And, multi-tasker that I am, I can do both simultaneously. Even while eating a candy bar. (Don't judge. It was chocolate. It's not like I had a choice.)

My husband doesn't judge. He doesn't tease me when I have a truckload of stapler-less staples or when I can't find something in my purse. One reason is that he's a really nice guy. I'm pretty sure the other reason is that he knows I see his office on a regular basis. Not that I'm comparing Richie's office to a junk drawer or to my purse or anything. Nevertheless I have to say, if he added nail polish, some lip gloss and a travel-sized can of hairspray, I could picture myself putting a shoulder strap on that office and hauling it to the mall to find shoes to match. We recently had to rummage through his office on a hunt for his keys. We searched high and low before we found them. I was glad to make it out of there in one piece. And without tetanus.

Search High and...High

Today I was also rummaging around in Scripture—though it was an entirely different kind of rummaging—and the word "seek" caught my attention. "Seek the LORD and his strength; seek his presence continually!" (Psalm 105:4). I may look for a stapler, look for a business card, look for a list, look for the keys—even look for the candy bar I didn't know I had. But no search is as vital as this one. It's a three-pronged search that I never, ever want to overlook. We're told to seek the Lord, seek

His strength and seek His presence. And to do this searching "continually."

It's a high search. To seek the Lord is to actively desire a connection with Him. It happens through reading His Word, through talking and listening to Him through prayer, through giving Him attention through worship—and through keeping fervent our desire to know Him more and more. These are the real and necessary staples of a victorious faith life. And despite what I said about how well I search for junk, this is no junk search. This is about the looking. And the never overlooking. Not multi-tasking. Singularly focused.

Seeking God's strength is recognizing that all might is His and that there's nothing we can do in this life without His empowering. Seeking His presence is understanding that He is in us and that He's at work around us. It's surrendering to Him, asking for His filling. It encompasses a stubbornly determined, unrelenting desire to love Him more completely and serve Him more passionately.

Jeremiah 29:11-13 confirms the need for whole-heartedness in our search. "For I know the plans I have for you, declares the LORD, plans for welfare and not for evil, to give you a future and a hope. Then you will call upon me and come and pray to me, and I will hear you. You will seek me and find me, when you seek me with all your heart."

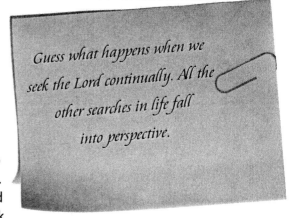

Guess what happens when we seek the Lord continually. All the other searches in life fall into perspective.

Some Solid Attachments

Guess what happens when we seek the Lord continually. All the other searches in life fall into perspective. That's a happy place—with or without the candy bar. The verse right before says, "Glory in his holy name; let the hearts of those who seek the LORD rejoice!" (Psalm 105:3).

A heart that's rightly seeking God is a heart that will rejoice. I want to glorify His holy name in the way that I seek. I want to be all about the looking. Never the overlooking. That's definitely a key element in a life well-lived.

Incidentally, any time you find a key element, you might want to make sure you don't leave it in my husband's office. Or my purse.

Sorting It Out

Look at Psalm 105:4 again: "Seek the Lord and his strength; seek his presence continually!" List some specific actions you can do to attach all three parts of this command to your life in a better-than-stapled way. You'll find several mentioned in this chapter. List those and any others the Lord might bring to your mind. Then pray through each one in surrender, asking for His filling and empowering to make them happen.

Specific ways to seek the Lord

_____
_____
_____
_____

Specific ways to seek His strength

_____
_____
_____
_____

Specific ways to seek His presence:

_____
_____
_____
_____

Ask the Lord to continue to inspire and empower your on-going "seeking" over the next weeks. Keep in mind His great love for you. No need to seek Him so He will love you more. He loves you to the max. But seek Him because He is worthy and let your worship be your wholehearted, all-in, soul-response. You might want to write Deuteronomy 4:29 on a card and place it somewhere you can see it often. Let it remind you to search—and search in the highest: "But from there you will seek the LORD your God and you will find him, if you search after him with all your heart and with all your soul."

chapter 3

Tissues: Tissue, Please

Kaley Rhea

Let this be recorded for a generation to come so that a people yet to be created may praise the LORD.
(Psalm 102:18)

I love how Monica has stories and messages and memories attached to so many of the items she's collected. Stories give value. Stories give meaning. What a powerful thing to be able to look at something physical, something with only the barest worldly worth, and make a connection to a past time or feeling or lesson. To give a *thing* a *story*. I can safely say this ability to experience an emotional or intellectual response to a rubber band or a handful of staples (or any of the other random objects you'll find in chapters 4-24) is one of the most special abilities the Lord has knit into us human beings.

Granted, I feel I can safely say this because I may be the least sentimental human being currently living.

I just don't get attached to things. First grade macaroni art? That was years ago; let's let this go. Backyard clubhouse my dad built? This thing is a rotting deathtrap; burn it. A great,

great aunt's collection of fabric scraps? Why do we even have this?

I'd like to be clear, this level of—apathy? Practicality? —is not something that comes standard in my family. My mom has been known to become attached to smudged fingerprints on her sliding glass door. ("Aw, look how tiny they are!") And I have a brother who became very upset when his childhood bedroom got tidied up, and he found someone had swept out a beloved ladybug carcass. ("I looked at it hanging over my bed every night before I went to sleep!") While I'm over here with a squirt bottle of Windex and a feather duster like *What is wrong with you people?*

Somebody—I hope—is reading this and nodding with me, thinking *Yes. Same.* But I know some of you are reading this and going *You cold-blooded monster,* and skipping ahead to read a Rhonda or Monica chapter. I don't blame you! At all! I know, okay? But bear with me a little longer. I promise it's about to get...*cute.*

There's Something in My Eye

My sister Allie has a one-year-old little girl named Emerson. Emerson and I, not to brag or anything, are buddies. She is a bright, clever, sunshiny kid, and all she wants to do all the time she's awake is *move.* Poor pumpkin was sick the other week, and when she's sick her mom puts the TV on to distract her and keep her from getting frustrated she can't move and play and dance exactly the way she wants.

So because we're buddies, Emerson and I, I sat on the floor with her while we watched a kiddie program and she touched everything in the room with her tiny chub hands. As we sat, I found myself getting pulled into this children's show. I don't know how it happened. There was a princess who was still learning how to be a princess, and her brother came through for her the way great brothers do, and I found myself getting choked up. Like I had to pause and take a moment. The emotions in a preschool animated musical got to be too much,

34

and I had to pull up and do some focused breathing. Me. The un-sentimentalist.

You know who teased me in that moment? Rhonda—Mom-Who-Gets-Emotionally-Attached-to-Fingerprints—Rhea, that's who. And Allie. Yeah, Allie teased me big time. You know who else? No one, because Emerson is an emotional person and showed a mature amount of empathy.

All right, it was kinda funny.

Emerson and I spent a lot of that evening tearing Kleenex into small pieces and complaining good-naturedly about our respective mothers. It occurred to me that I did not become affected when I saw a picture of that animated princess. My eyes didn't well up when I read the show's description. Or when I learned her name. Nothing about that silly show came anywhere close to touching me on an emotional level until I learned her story. Until I saw her struggle. Until I knew her kind little princess heart.

I do not connect very well or very often to *things*. But I can connect to a *story*.

Tell Me Another

Do you wonder sometimes about the different ways God could've chosen to relate to us? He could have said "I am God, and you are human. Worship me." And that would've been right and just. But we wouldn't have known Him. If He wanted to, He could have said, "If you possess this amulet or such and such trinket, or say these words to this statue, you may know my favor." But He didn't.

He gave us His story.

At the end of the apostle John's gospel account, he wrote, "Jesus performed many other signs in the presence of his disciples that are not written in this book. But these are written so that you may believe that Jesus is the Messiah, the Son of God, and that by believing you may have life in his name (John 20:30-31 CSB)."

From the beginning of time, through the Old Testament, to the cross, in the resurrection, to the revelation, God loves us so much, has such a desire to connect with us, that He wrote it down. The places. The people. The evidence. The truth. Does that blow your mind? That blows my mind! Sometimes I get so caught up in mining the Bible for "What is right in this situation?" and "How does this apply to my life?" that I miss the joy of being swept up by God's own history. I forget to marvel over and revel in the God who is present in every page, in every story, in every moment He chose specially to preserve for millennia so my tiny human mind could process even a fraction of an understanding of who Jesus Christ is. Deep breath.

Am I getting emotional now? Emerson, get the tissues!

I'm Not Crying, You're Crying

Several days after Allie and Emerson went home from that visit, Allie sent a video of Emerson playing with a bunch of tissues. She had several of those travel packs everybody keeps one or two of in their junk drawers. My little buddy was grinning and arranging them and patting them like they'd done a good job. Allie said something like, "She doesn't know what these are. But she knows they make us feel better."

It reminded me first of the night of quality time tearing up tissues with my buddy. And second it reminded me how I first came to learn about Jesus. Through Bible stories. Through people who loved me enough to share them with me so I could understand, so I could connect. Stories and words the Holy Spirit graciously used to draw me to Himself.

And it reminded me of this verse, John 13:35, "By this all people will know that you are my disciples, if you have love for one another." It made me think of all the someones in the world looking for hope in their own stories. It made me pray they would see a Christian who loves so well that that lost person thinks, "I don't know what this is, but I know it makes me feel better. And I want to know more."

So thanks for that, Emerson.

It's important for me, as a person too often frustrated by emotions—my own and others' emotions—to remember that deep, satisfying, emotional connection is a gift. And while in a fallen world where emotions can so easily be manipulated from a million different sin-corrupted directions, there is wisdom in not trusting all feelings. But emotions are a part of who God is. And He wants us to use emotions rightly. Relationship is part of who God is. And when He made us in His image, how incredible that He chose to share emotions and relationship with us!

What we have is not a religion of relics we have to search out. What we have is not a boss wearing a nametag, or a lord bearing a title instead of providing an introduction. We have God who gave us His stories. We have a Friend who invites us to know Him. We have a Father who proves He has known us since before we knew anything.

That gets to this cold-hearted monster's heart every time.

"Let this be recorded for a generation to come, so that a people yet to be created may praise the Lord: that he looked down from his holy height; from heaven the LORD looked at the earth, to hear the groans of the prisoners, to set free those who were doomed to die, that they may declare in Zion the name of the LORD, and in Jerusalem his praise, when peoples gather together, and kingdoms, to worship the LORD" (Psalm 102:18-22).

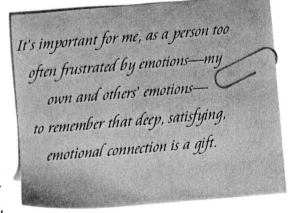

It's important for me, as a person too often frustrated by emotions—my own and others' emotions— to remember that deep, satisfying, emotional connection is a gift.

Sorting It Out

What is your favorite story from the Bible? What about it generates emotion in you or is otherwise especially meaningful to you? What is it that you personally connect with?

_____
_____
_____

Tell a story from your life. A moment you felt the presence of God or He provided in exactly the way you needed. You can even start it with "Once upon a time" if you like. (Although apparently if you include any princesses, I may get weepy.)

_____
_____
_____

1 Peter 3:15 reads, "But in your hearts honor Christ the Lord as holy, always being prepared to make a defense to anyone who asks you for a reason for the hope that is in you; yet do it with gentleness and respect." A great way to honor Jesus is by studying His Word—learning His story so well you can share it with anyone who hasn't heard or doesn't understand it. Let's practice! Jot down a few reasons for the hope that is in you. What can you say if someone asks you, "Why Jesus?"

_____
_____
_____

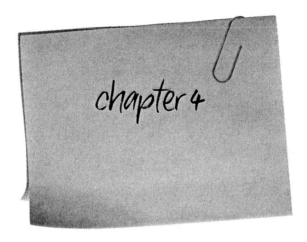

Tape Measure: Measuring Ourselves by God's Word

Monica Schmelter

And her rival used to provoke her grievously
to irritate her, because the LORD
had closed her womb.
(I Samuel 1:6)

I found two tape measures in my junk drawer. I think that's odd because I don't use a tape measure very often. Even when I do use a tape measure I am not always as exact as I need to be. I think that's why I usually must order curtains twice before they fit properly.

As a teenager I was really good at measuring myself against others and coming up short. No one had to teach me how to do that. I didn't even have to measure twice. I just looked around and thought things like: "She is prettier than me," "She is a smarter than me," and there was always "She is thinner than me."

I was obsessed with the scale as a teenager. Being thin was very important to my family and to me. I can't tell you how many times I wondered how I could be born into a family of thin people while I struggled with being overweight. This was just one area that I measured myself against others and came up short.

In hindsight I realize my families' extreme concern with weight was dysfunctional. After Sunday dinner all of the women and teen girls (immediate and extended family) would go into the living room and weigh in. As we took turns stepping on the scale our weight would be announced and recorded in a blue spiral notebook. For me this was a tradition of torturous proportions. Everyone in our group except me weighed less than 110 pounds with shoes and after Sunday dinner.

Really Mean Girls

During several weigh-in sessions I secretly prayed to pass out. God never answered this crazy prayer but that didn't stop me from asking. I desperately wanted out of the weekly weigh-in with relatives who I would describe as really mean girls.

Really mean girls (RMG from here on out) are not a modern phenomenon. Peninnah (pronounced pee-NIHN-uh) was one of first really mean girls in the Bible. Peninnah was married to Elkanah. Hannah was also married to Elkanah. Yes you read that correctly—one husband with two wives. Peninnah and Hannah may very well be the first Sister Wives in the Bible.

Peninnah frequently taunted Hannah to the point of tears. Often she did this on their way to worship. Peninnah used her childbearing abilities to provoke Hannah. When childless Hannah held her tape measure up against the baby-maker Peninnah, she believed she came up short.

We Are Masterpieces

When we measure ourselves against others we are essentially reducing our value to a number on the scale, a grade on a report card, a bank account statement, and the list goes on. The reading of our tape measure can be deceitful and cruel. The reading of God's Word unveils our true value. He says that we are his masterpieces (Ephesians 2:10, NLT) and that out of all creation we (people) are His most prized possession.

When we believe what the world says about how we measure up, we call God a liar. Of course we don't mean to call God a liar. It's just the we've heard so many comments about what a woman should be and stepped on so many scales that we've gotten confused.

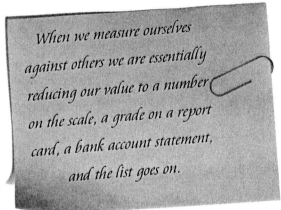

When we measure ourselves against others we are essentially reducing our value to a number on the scale, a grade on a report card, a bank account statement, and the list goes on.

In my teen years, I wanted to be thin. I felt that if I could just lose 30 or so pounds that I would measure up to my families' and friends' expectations. The weekly family weigh-in didn't last forever but it wasn't over soon enough for me. As long as I measured myself by their standards I came up short, lonely, and filled with unnecessary shame.

Perhaps you measure yourself by what other people say and expect. Maybe you have a friend or family member who is your Peninnah. There are people who seem to specialize in taunting others. I call these sorts of people High Maintenance (HM for short).

A Painful Dilemma

What to do in a world filled with Peninnahs and tape measures? We can learn a lesson from Hannah who sought help for her painful dilemma. She didn't enlist Elkanah's help, perhaps because he totally missed the point (1 Samuel 1:8). She took her problem to God in prayer.

It was to Him that Hannah poured out her heart. She cried so hard during one prayer session that a priest thought she was drunk. That's one ugly, messy cry. If you know her story you know that God answered her prayer and gave her a son.

The taunts of the RMG named Peninnah drove Hannah to her knees in prayer. We all face painful situations. We can either live with the pain of measuring ourselves against others or allow the very things that make us feel weak to bring us to prayer.

The Great Exchange

Talking to God is an essential part of learning who we are in Christ. A great exchange occurs when we take our weaknesses to God in prayer. Let's look at how God responded to one of Paul's requests: "My grace is sufficient for you, for my power is made perfect in weakness" (2 Corinthians 12:9).

God responded to Paul by saying His power is made perfect in weakness. In this particular situation God didn't grant Paul's request exactly the way he prayed it. Instead God told Paul that His grace was sufficient.

Sometimes that is how God answers us as well. He doesn't always remove the Peninnahs and tape measures from our lives. But He will (if we let Him) give us strength for every challenge, solutions for every problem, healing for every cutting remark, and the kind of love that covers a multitude of sins.

A great exchange occurs when we take our weaknesses to God in prayer.

I definitely perceived my extra pounds as a deficiency of epic proportions. I feared that I'd never have a boyfriend or get married. I endured relentless shaming from some of my family members and friends. Their harsh comments only reinforced what I already feared.

As it turns out I did get married. After 4 years of marriage God blessed us with a wonderful son. But even as a grown woman I secretly struggled with not measuring up to my own or others' expectations. Whether at church or the store I quietly compared myself with others. When I held up my tape measure, I came up short every single time.

The Discrepancy

By outward appearances I had a good life. My husband and I had a good relationship. Our son was healthy. I was a stay at home mom, and I led Bible studies at church. I knew there was a discrepancy between what God's Word said about me and how I felt—I just wasn't sure what to do about it.

As the years passed, I started getting invitations to speak at women's conferences. I was also asked to host a daily Christian television program. Even with all these blessings my secret struggle continued. I finally decided to pray about my secret struggle. Answers didn't come right away but over time I developed a new perspective. As I prayed, I read verses like these:

> "Are not five sparrows sold for two pennies? And not one of them is forgotten before God. Why, even the hairs of your head are all numbered. Fear not; you are of more value than many sparrows" (Luke 12:6-8).

> "But let your adorning be the hidden person of the heart with the imperishable beauty of a gentle and quiet spirit, which in God's sight is very precious" (1 Peter 3:4).

As I read these verses and others, I had a fresh understanding of how much God loved me and what was valuable in His sight. The more I embraced His love for me the less inclined I was to measure myself against other people.

Where Was That Blue Spiral Notebook?

This doesn't mean that I am never tempted anymore to compare myself to others. Several years ago I found myself sitting at the kitchen table with some of the RMGs, the same women who headed up the weekly weigh-in. Let's just say all of them had gained a considerable amount of weight and that I was 70 pounds lighter. For a brief moment, I thought about grabbing the scale and asking all of them to weigh in. Where was that blue spiral notebook anyway? Thankfully, I was able to regain my sanity and rest in what I know to be true. My value—your value—is not determined by a number on the scale. Our value comes from our Creator and He says we are fearfully and wonderfully made. We are GORGEOUS!

Just as You Are

God is the only one who knows our true value. When we believe His Word over this world's system, we can walk in wholeness and peace. He loves us just because we are His. We can put our tape measure back in the junk drawer and rest in the knowledge that God loves us radically—just the way we are.

Sorting It Out

List some areas where you measure yourself against others.

_____

_____

_____

In what areas do you think you come up short?

_____

_____

_____

List some verses that will help you see yourself as God does.

_____

_____

_____

When we measure our value by God's Word we never come up short. It's up to us to put down our tape measure and let God's Word have the final say.

chapter 5

Spare Change: If I Had a Nickel for Every Change

Rhonda Rhea

*And I will give you a new heart, and a new
spirit I will put within you. And I will remove
the heart of stone from your flesh and give you
a heart of flesh.*
(Ezekiel 36:26)

If I had a nickel for every time I said I needed to clean out that junk drawer... Oh wait. I sort of do. It seems I have all the nickels right here in the drawer. And most of the dimes. And boatloads of pennies. Loads and loads and then more loads of pennies. Not that many quarters. Those would actually be useful. But the other coins, oh yes.

Every once in a while at my house, we gather up all those nickels, dimes, and pennies. We invest them. Not in stocks or bonds or anything like that. No, we invest in a project or a cause that appreciates spare change. Someone's car wash. A mission project. A pan of brownies.

I know what you're thinking. A pan of brownies is not usually considered an investment. Or a mission. But I consider it a positive action I can take for my health's sake so maybe we could think of it as both. Sort of. Again, I know what you're thinking. I am not unconvinced, however, that brownies can't be part of my workout. I tried it just today. My workout routine for this afternoon: stirred brownie batter. I'm pretty sure I was sweating because it was especially thick brownie batter. So thick I'm probably going to need a nap. Right after I eat a couple of these brownies.

Changing the Way I Think?

I'll hurry to warn you that for people like me who call brownie-stirring a workout, the abs tend to end up about the same consistency as that brownie batter. It's both fascinating and gross. It's hard for me to look at my abs and not think to myself that something should probably change.

Didn't I read somewhere I could think myself thin? In that vein, I think I'll plan some imaginary cardio for later this afternoon. Of course, for all of us who plan to think our exercise, abs of batter will probably always be our buns of steel.

While we're thinking about it, how about a reminder to put more than just thought into our faith life? An intellectual exercise alone will do about as much for our spiritual wellbeing as imaginary exercise will do for us physically.

Maybe you've read Romans 12:1-2 even more times than I've dodged my workouts. I read it routinely. And though I read it routinely, it's always a heart-charger. And a heart-changer. Like spiritual cardio, this passage so often becomes a faith workout routine for my heart and mind: "Therefore, brothers, by the mercies of God, I urge you to present your bodies as a living sacrifice, holy and pleasing to God; this is your spiritual worship. Do not be conformed to this age, but be transformed by the renewing of your mind, so that you may discern what is the good, pleasing, and perfect will of God" (HCSB).

Change of Heart, Soul, Mind—All

That's the kind of spiritual cardio that is truly heart-changing. No nickel and dime stuff here. We're talking about the kind of change that counts. I'm reminded in this passage to present my body, brownies and all. And I'm reminded to let my mind be renewed too. Both are exercises of obedience. Both are exercises of faith. The Lord wants our bodies. He wants our minds. He wants us heart, soul—absolutely all. He wants us in the most complete, scrape-every-part-of-the-bowl way.

Following Him is not merely an intellectual exercise. It's verified in our sacrifice. It's at the point of total surrender that we're free to understand, to "discern," the "perfect will of God" (Romans 12:2).

> *O Lord, may we be ever-ready to give body, mind, heart and soul to You and lovingly follow.*

Spare Change?

In one sense, there's no real spare change. Only change. No one is spared. No one minute is like the last. With every new minute we have a whole new slate of decisions to make. "How will I live?" The biggest question of all is, "Will I allow the Lord to work in and through me?" Folded into that question are, "Will I allow my mind and body—everything I think and everything I am—to be placed on the altar?" "Will I follow Him?" "Will I let the work of His Holy Spirit change me?" This is an entirely different kind of

In one sense, there's no real spare change. Only change. No one is spared.

change. And it leads to an entirely different kind of life—one that's energized with purpose.

The instant we become His, there is a marvelous, magnificent change. "Therefore, if anyone is in Christ, he is a new creation. The old has passed away; behold, the new has come" (2 Corinthians 5:17).

Let's be crystal clear on this one important point. "In Christ" is key in that passage. We can resolve and try and promise and work and squirm to change ourselves. But it will never happen. Real change only happens as we allow the Lord to do it in us. That's the truth.

On the other hand, as far as the change in the junk drawer is concerned, if you have some too, I was just thinking maybe you could pool it all together and buy a box of brownies. You know. For exercise purposes.

Sorting It Out

Look at that verse in 2 Corinthians in the Amplified Version: "Therefore if anyone is in Christ [that is, grafted in, joined to Him by faith in Him as Savior], *he is* a new creature [reborn and renewed by the Holy Spirit]; the old things [the previous moral and spiritual condition] have passed away. Behold, new things have come [because spiritual awakening brings a new life]" (2 Corinthians 5:17, AMP).

Write it out, inserting your name in the "anyone" spot. Substitute your name for "he" too. You. You are a new creature. He has all power to change you in Christ.

_____
_____
_____
_____
_____
_____

Paul said, "And I am sure of this, that he who began a good work in you will bring it to completion at the day of Jesus

Christ" (Philippians 1:6) How does understanding this truth affect how you look at change? How does it affect how you experience change?

_____

_____

_____

_____

_____

_____

How might these thoughts on change change the way your week looks?

_____

_____

_____

"And we all, with unveiled face, beholding the glory of the Lord, are being transformed into the same image from one degree of glory to another. For this comes from the Lord who is the Spirit" (2 Corinthians 3:18).

chapter 6

Buttons: Learning to Button It

Kaley Rhea

*Let no corrupting talk come out of your
mouths, but only such as is good for building
up, as fits the occasion, that it may give
grace to those who hear.*
(Ephesians 4:29)

High-waisted pants are in right now, and I love it. I know in making this declaration I'm running the risk of dating this book terribly. In a few months or years, will someone read this and think, *Wow, those late two-thousand teens were a fashion disaster*? Maybe. Will that person be me? It's not unlikely. But I grew up in the 90s; so I've made plenty of peace with all kinds of unfortunate wardrobe scenarios.

While I freely acknowledge my love for my high-waisted jeans, I will say there is one downside. The buttons. There. Are. So. Many. Which isn't a huge problem except A: You finally get inside the stall during a bathroom emergency, and your pants seem so complicated it feels like you have to defuse a bomb ("Come on, come on! I only got fifteen seconds left! Everyone clear the area!"), and B: You're between three and five times more likely to lose a button.

And when I lose a button, let me tell you, the pants will go out of style long before I get around to sewing on a new one.

Fixing a button simply isn't on my radar and never quite makes it to my to-do list. I've been shown how to sew on a button (Thanks, Mom). I have the supplies necessary for sewing on a button (Again, Mom, thanks). But I'm not in the habit of getting out needle and thread. As many times as I've thought, "I should put a button on that," I've never made it a priority in my life. I mean, I tend to buy like $12 pants. What's the point?

Sew What?

I've noticed I can be like that with speaking kindly. I know how to do it. I have the supplies necessary. People around me also seem to want to teach their children to be kind—to share, to say sweet words, and to play nice. But between you and me, my fellow grownups, we can be some real sass-mouth kids to each other. Like we don't always make kindness a priority. Like we haven't seen the value. Or the point..

Super-broadly speaking as a culture, we're way too inclined to celebrate the zingers. The quick come-backs, the high-brow insults, the comedic teasing. Something in us loves to shout, "Ohhhh! Apply cool water to that burn!" after a particularly germane gibe. We like to laugh. And a lot of times, we really mean it all in fun.

The problem—in addition to the possibility of hurting someone's feelings—is that this pattern of speaking can be habit-forming. Has it become weird to look someone in the face and speak sincerely some kind words to them? Or to hear kind words spoken to you? Words you can trust? The truth is, we can so thoroughly train our brains in this method of verbal sparring that we look to score empty points with hardly a conscious thought—while trying to honestly encourage someone is like trying to do calligraphy wrong-handed. It's uncomfortable. And it probably doesn't turn out like what you had in mind.

But Ephesians 4:32 tells us to, "Be kind to one another, tenderhearted..." Those of you who have ever been a child, what could be sweeter to you than seeing kiddos show kindness to you? Have you thought about ways you can bless your heavenly Father lately? Here's a great one! Be kind. Be tenderhearted. Where there may be discomfort or awkwardness or an odd feeling of vulnerability in the effort to replace glibness with kindness, don't give up. Think of your yearning to hear words like this. Put yourself in the other's shoes and think tenderly of what you'd want or need. Think of Jesus and this opportunity you have to be sweet to Him.

Kindness is dismissing the desire to put someone in their place, and instead asking the Lord to use you however He wants in that moment, that you might see someone else victorious in Christ.

I think sometimes we get the idea that a kind and thoughtful person is this saccharine, obnoxious, boring, weak, or false sort of person. So let's be clear. Kindness isn't the same as lying or flattering or overlooking sin. In fact, sometimes confrontation is the kind thing to do. Psalm 141:5 says, "Let a righteous man strike me—it is a kindness; let him rebuke me—it is oil for my head; let my head not refuse it."

Replacing truth with feel-goodisms is no kind of kindness at all. It's more like apathy in fact. At best. Manipulation at worst. It distances us from people just like celebrating the zingers. But real kindness is genuine. It requires approaching someone in love and with the understanding that you are not their superior. That their struggle could just as easily be yours. It pulls the two of you together.

Thread Lightly

There is another something a bit sinister in the habitual barbing: it tends to keep things on a superficial level. It's difficult to share personal struggles or victories or vices with someone whose tendency is to laugh things off or call things out. So even if sharp-but-seemingly-funny insults are the popular thing, they're not generally what people are thirsting for.

We may celebrate the wit of the jokesters, but we are drawn to the hearts of the kind. Probably because when people are being kind, they're being like Jesus. Like Galatians 5:22-23 says, "But the fruit of the Spirit is love, joy, peace, patience, kindness, goodness, faithfulness, gentleness, self-control; against such things there is no law."

Kindness is an evidence of the work of the Holy Spirit in you. If you find yourself defaulting to caustic put-downs or casual brush-offs, ask Him to change your mind. Ask Him to show you how to bless Him by blessing others with your truly-fun-and-funny words and actions. Keep in mind God's the one who designed laughter. Making people laugh is awesome. No one has to be cruel to be funny.

Don't make the mistake of believing that kindness is a lesson we ought to reserve for children. It's massively important. It's a command. It's central to life. It draws us close to people. And it's impossible to do it well without the help of our tirelessly kind and merciful Father.

> We may celebrate the wit of the jokesters, but we are drawn to the hearts of the kind.

And by the way, just as an aside: I hope someone does read this in like 2075 and thinks "Whoa, high-waisted pants! I should bring those back again!" and launches a fashion revolution. I think I can have my button sewn back on by then. Maybe.

Sorting It Out

How can you take kindness out of the Sunday school classroom and make it really work in real life?

_____

_____

_____

I'm going to drop three heavy verses on us right here.

"If anyone thinks he is religious and does not bridle his tongue but deceives his heart, this person's religion is worthless" (James 1:26).

"Let your speech always be gracious, seasoned with salt, so that you may know how you ought to answer each person" (Colossians 4:6).

"You brood of vipers! How can you speak good, when you are evil? For out of the abundance of the heart the mouth speaks" (Matthew 12:34).

That last verse from Matthew—that's Jesus speaking. Getting real with some Pharisees—the religious elite of the day. Back story: they'd just seen Jesus casting out demons, just heard the people wondering if He really is the promised Savior, and so they started talking trash about how Jesus must get his power from the devil. And Jesus basically told them they're a bunch of snakes. Their kind of slander is exactly Satan's M.O. It's so convicting to me because sometimes that's me! Sometimes that's even me at church. We do that, right? We use our words to devour each other, to spit venom, to be the opposite of loving, the opposite of kind, the opposite of the God we say we serve. How often do we speak caustically to believers, and so sabotage our purpose and community? How often do the lost and the searching peek in at us, listen to our barbed words and think, What a worthless religion. Breaks my heart.

Is there anyone in your life you've gotten in the habit of speaking ungraciously to or about? Take a moment to confess that to the Lord. Ask him to rewire your thinking and your mouth, to override that habit. And then write some kind things about that person in particular. Nothing empty or flattering. But something true and good and thoughtful. Even if the only positive you can think of while remaining honest in your heart is "God created them" or "God loves them." Start there.

_____

_____

_____

Now, think of someone you love! Someone you admire and respect. Write down why, just for fun. Gush a little. Be proud and grateful and, even knowing their faults and flaws celebrate the reasons you treasure them. Write the good things you've told them often or the things you never have. Find a place in your week to drop some of those things into your conversation with your person.

_____

_____

_____

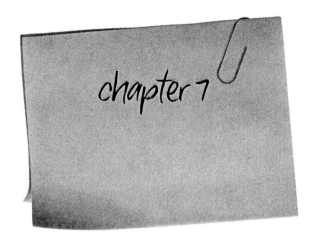

chapter 7

Duct Tape: When a Quick Fix Is Not Quick and Doesn't Fix

Monica Schmelter

Come to me, all who labor and are heavy laden, and I will give you rest.
(Matthew 11:28)

It started out innocently enough. While I was rushing to walk out the door to speak at a women's meeting I noticed a thread dangling from my skirt. I tugged at the thread and to my dismay the entire hem unraveled. With no time to change I headed for my junk drawer where I found a quick fix.

While I was at the women's meeting I received many compliments on my outfit. I interpreted that to mean that no one knew the hem of my skirt was secured with duct tape. It was a temporary fix that worked fabulously in my moment of need.

Some of my earliest memories involve me trying to fix things. When I was in pre-school I tried to fix a broken crayon with glue. I tried to fix my parents broken marriage by being the perfect little girl. I wasn't successful in either of those endeavors but that didn't stop me from trying.

It Didn't Take Long

Over the years I developed my fix-it skills to the point that I offered advice to anyone who would listen. In most cases the person would listen and then turn around and do something else. It didn't take long for me to find the fix it-thing to be exhausting.

When I met my friend, who I'll call Renee,* I immediately recognized that she also liked to be an expert of sorts at fixing people.

> Over the years I developed my fix-it skills to the point that I offered advice to anyone who would listen.

As we sipped lattes, I listened as Renee tried to fix co-workers, church friends, and her grown daughter Shae.*

It was her concern for Shae that caught my attention and prayers.

What I understand from Renee (and, yes, I do change names to protect privacy and redemption but the story is true) was that Shae was a bright and outgoing child. Shae made friends easily, but struggled with insecurities, and didn't do well in school. While she was capable of completing her schoolwork she rarely did. When Renee was notified by teachers about missing assignments she would jump in and finish the work so Shae could get a passing grade. Renee justified her actions by saying she was only helping.

Failure to Complete Assignments

Renee's husband watched from a distance and offered little help. While he loved his daughter very much, he had a basic it-will-all-work-out-in-the-end sort of attitude. Renee resented his lackadaisical attitude, and she and her husband argued frequently. They argued about other things too. Sometimes it got physical. Shae witnessed all of this, and Renee suspected that this was the root cause of Shae's insecurity and failure to complete assignments. Even so, Renee painted a happy picture of her marriage.

This pattern continued through Shae's high school years. After high school graduation Shae was unclear and unprepared to make plans for the future. Shortly after graduation she started to hang out with a different group of people and began taking drugs.

One day Renee and her husband asked Shae to be home by noon for a visit with her grandparents. Shae promised to be home in time. On the day of the visit Shae showed up about 2 PM. When Shae walked in the front door Renee knew she was high or altered.

Bad Reaction to Medicine?

Once again Renee jumped in to rescue. She made up an excuse that Shae wasn't feeling well and having a bad reaction to medicine. Renee made apologies for Shae and worked to fix the situation as best she could.

A few months later, Shae announced that she was moving in with friends. Renee and her husband expressed their concern since Shae didn't have any income. Shae assured them she would get a job quickly. She reminded them that she was an adult, and there was nothing they could do to stop her.

Renee did her best to smile through the move. When friends and family asked about Shae, Renee painted a happy picture. Inside Renee was filled with fear and prayed many silent prayers. She had done her best with Shae and tried so hard to keep her on the straight and narrow. Despite Renee's best efforts and silent prayers, nothing Renee did to fix Shae, or even point her in the right direction, worked.

Mother/Daughter Time

Several months later Renee was elated when Shae asked her to come to visit for a few days. Shae explained her roommate would be on vacation so it would be a perfect time to enjoy some mother-daughter time. When Renee arrived at Shae's house she knew something was wrong. Shae looked very thin and pale and was slurring her words. The refrigerator was empty and past due bills littered the kitchen table. Renee feared her daughter was using drugs again.

When Renee told Shae what she was thinking Shae said, "Mom, I assure you that I am not doing anything wrong." Renee wanted to believe that but the signs were all there.

Later that evening Renee's fears were confirmed when she found her daughter lying in bed with a straw in her hand and white powder on a small plate. With tears in her eyes, Renee grabbed the straw and picked up the plate with white powder and said, "I cannot allow you to do this." Shae remained silent.

Over the next few days, Renee begged Shae to get help. She even set up a few counseling appointments on her daughter's behalf. Shae refused to go. Renee called her husband and a few close friends and asked them to pray.

Where Had She Gone Wrong?

When it was time for Renee to leave she pleaded with Shae to come home with her. Shae was adamant she wasn't going anywhere. As Renee drove home her mind raced in a million directions. Where had she gone wrong? Was she too strict? Not strict enough?

When Renee arrived home she told her husband the whole sordid story. Her normally quiet husband said, "This time we should let her experience the consequences of her own actions." Renee was frustrated by his response but said nothing.

Later, one of Renee's close friends called and said, "You need to put your daughter in God's hands. You have done everything you can do. Only God can fix this." That wasn't music to Renee's ears but deep in her heart she suspected her husband and friend might be right.

Renee decided to see a Christian counselor that specialized in working with families with substance abuse issues.

During her first appointment she let her guard down and was surprised at how freeing it was to be honest. After several sessions Renee was able to see with clarity her need to rescue and save her daughter from unpleasant consequences.

With the help of a counselor and a support group Renee learned how to rest in the Lord. A very familiar Bible verse became personal to Renee: "Come to me, all who labor and are heavy laden, and I will give you rest" (Matthew 11:28). While she loved and prayed for her daughter daily, she resisted the temptation to rescue and enable.

Full-blown Addiction

Renee made a commitment to stop fixing and trust God in new ways. This included taking every fearful and worried thought captive. When the urge to rescue her daughter surfaced, she stopped, prayed, and called one of her trusted friends for support

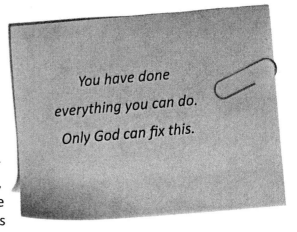

You have done everything you can do. Only God can fix this.

Renee's journey to freedom accelerated when she realized all of her fixes were only temporary, and sometimes even worked against the solution. Her efforts to rescue Shae from consequences only delayed the inevitable. What started as doing her daughter's homework in elementary school grew into covering a full-blown addiction for Renee.

While it was painful for Renee to face the truth it was incredibly freeing to stop the façade. When Renee told her husband what she was learning in counseling, she was surprised at his response. He said that watching her reach out for help inspired him to be more honest about his feelings. He said that he thought he needed counseling too.

It took several months before Shae was ready for help. She joined Celebrate Recovery, A Christ-centered recovery program, and started to make progress. Part of Shae's recovery included moving back home with her parents. This time Renee and her husband talked with Shae together. The three of them came up with a plan with healthy boundaries and well-defined expectations and consequences. There was a huge learning curve for all of them but day by day they worked it out.

Shae has been clean and sober for five years now. She graduated from college and entered the work force full time. This time when she moved out her parents were involved and supportive.

With God's Help

There are still occasions when Renee worries about her daughter relapsing. Every once in a while Renee's husband becomes silent and has to be encouraged to open up. Shae is sometimes tempted to use. What they all learned is that, with God's help, we can skip temporary fixes and receive true healing. They also treasure each moment and look for opportunities to celebrate their many blessings and freedom in Christ.

Sorting it Out

What are areas in your life that you try to fix?

_____

_____

_____

What would it look like for you to let go of the temporary fix and trust God for lasting change?

_____

_____

_____

What can you do this week that will get you on your journey to trusting God for lasting change?

_____
_____
_____

chapter 8

Bread Ties: Tying Up Our Hungers Well

Rhonda Rhea

O God, you are my God; earnestly I seek
you; my soul thirsts for you.
(Psalm 63:1)

That drawer. It's messy. No denying that. But I like to point out (often and loudly) that other people have junk drawers messier than mine. I know that's an immature response. I do. Nevertheless, *Hey! Look at that other person's messy drawer!*

I remember my grandma's junk drawer fondly. She was a great woman, yes. But the reason I remember her junk drawer so fondly is that thinking about hers makes me feel good about mine. It wasn't the overall messiness that made it a wild junk drawer. Her drawer was semi-organized and at least fairly often made some kind of sense, as far as junk drawers go. Except for the bread ties. That's where sense ended and the weird took over. Oh, the bread ties.

Those little flexy-plastic-covered wiry things. She saved them all. All. But for what? When did we ever, EV-er, reuse one? For anything? We barely ever even used them to tie up the bread bag.

I'm pretty sure my grandma had one of those little bread wires for every loaf of bread ever consumed the entire time I was growing up. We still don't know why.

When you take a wire and then cover it with flexy-plastic, does it suddenly become too nice a product to throw away? Grandma was anything but wasteful. And chock-full of ingenuity, that woman. It wouldn't surprise me to learn Grandma had plans to weave them into tools. Maybe tools for making suspension bridges or something awesome like that. She had so many of them she might've actually had enough for the suspension bridge too.

The part of the bread tie story that might entertain me the most is the memory that Grandma hardly ever used them to cinch up the bread bag. We were one of those families who could eat a loaf of bread faster than it could go stale. The only thing we ate faster than bread was cake.

The Tool of Drool

I never saw a stale cake in my home. I obviously passed that cake gene on to my children. You're going to think I'm making this up, but I had this very conversation with Kaley some months back:

Kaley: "Know what I found just now on Pinterest? Peanut butter cup gooey butter cake."

Me: "I just gained three pounds hearing you speak those words."

Kaley: "I just lost three pounds in drool."

After I thought about it—well, after I laughed for several minutes, and *then* after I thought about it—I decided she might actually have something there. The next diet craze? How about "Slobber Yourself Thin!"

I don't know why that shouldn't work for even an over-the-top cake-eater like me. Show me an even half-decent fudge cake, and suddenly I'm a St. Bernard.

On the new diet plan, it wouldn't even matter that I'm not the greatest cook in town. Nothing would depend on my baking. Just other people's pictures of theirs. Seems to me as long as there is social media, finding food snapshots won't be a problem. Log on any medium, and there's a virtual slobber-azzi.

I'm intrigued by the exercise implications here too. Instead of the tying on the tennies for running—and easier than tying on a bread tie—I could just tie on the drool bib. Ready, set, salivate!

Who knew drool could be a strategic tool in the arsenal of weight loss weapons? I think I'll start a board on Pinterest for all my spittle-inducing photos. Kaley said I should call it "Pavlov's Pics." ...That does ring a bell.

Dinner Bell or Sinner Bell?

But you know what rings truer? The reality of our spiritual appetites. I have to ask myself regularly what my soul might be drooling after. In this fallen world, the temptation is always there: hunger for possessions or position, thirst for enjoyment or ease.

Our enemy whispers in our ear, enticing our focus away from things eternal to everything temporary and ultimately unsatisfying.

Our souls are created to be thirsty. The problem is that we so often go after all the wrong things to quench that thirst.

Our souls are created to be thirsty. The problem is that we so often go after all the wrong things to quench that thirst. We head for the temporary substitutes that leave us more spiritually dehydrated than ever. Sometimes we compare our hungers and thirsts with those around us. I suppose I can feel good about myself when someone else is messier than I am. "Look at that other person's mess." Not exactly the mature response. Because the fact is, I can't be hungry or thirsty on behalf of anyone else. Just me.

Isn't it funny, though, that as we choose to stay hungry and thirsty for the Lord, we're satisfied? In Matthew 5:6 Jesus promised, "Blessed are those who hunger and thirst for righteousness, for they shall be satisfied." Hungry and thirsty. Yet at the same time, completely satisfied. Our thirst—our longing for Him and His ways—can be a tool in the hand of God, shaping us into the image of Christ by His Holy Spirit. As we're reminded of our desperate need for Him and as we ask Him to fill us, any other thing we ever craved make so much less sense. He is absolutely all we need.

Stay Thirsty, Pray Thirsty

David prayed thirsty in the verse at the first of this chapter: "O God, you are my God; earnestly I seek you; my soul thirsts for you" (Psalm 63:l).

Just a few verses later, we're given a delicious description of what happens after a hungry/thirsty prayer: "My soul will be satisfied as with fat and rich food, and my mouth will praise you with joyful lips" (Psalm 63:5).

That leaves me feeling wonderfully full, in the most real-to-the-soul way. Jesus said in John 7:37-38, "If anyone thirsts, let him come to me and drink. Whoever believes in me, as the Scripture has said, 'Out of his heart will flow rivers of living water.'"

Father, Son, and Holy Spirit—we are complete in our triune God who meets our every need as we hunger and thirst for Him.

No fooling. And definite drooling.

"Now on the last and most important day of the feast, Jesus stood and called out [in a loud voice], "If anyone is thirsty, let him come to Me and drink! He who believes in Me [who adheres to, trusts in, and relies on Me], as the Scripture has said, 'From his innermost being

will flow *continually* rivers of living water.'"
John 7:37-38 AMP

Sorting It Out:

Psalm 63 tells us so much about hungering and thirsting well. As you look at these eight verses, underline sections and make some notes about actions the psalmist took that would influence how a person lives, thinks, hungers, thirsts.

> "O God, you are my God; earnestly I seek you; my soul thirsts for you; my flesh faints for you, as in a dry and weary land where there is no water. So I have looked upon you in the sanctuary, beholding your power and glory. Because your steadfast love is better than life, my lips will praise you. So I will bless you as long as I live; in your name I will lift up my hands. My soul will be satisfied as with fat and rich food,and my mouth will praise you with joyful lips, when I remember you upon my bed, and meditate on you in the watches of the night; for you have been my help, and in the shadow of your wings I will sing for joy.My soul clings to you; your right hand upholds me"
> (Psalm 63:1-8).

Write out your personal hungry/thirsty plan of action based on the passage:

_____

_____

_____

_____

_____

_____

Are there hungers and thirsts in your life that have been leading you away from the Lord instead of inspiring you to seek Him? Write out a prayer of surrender. Ask Him to replace those desires with Spirit-led hungers.

_____

_____

_____

Write out some beautiful ways the Lord has enabled you to hunger and thirst well. How has hungering and thirsting well satisfied you like nothing else? How has it shown you what to do even in the trickiest of situations?

_____

_____

_____

"Oh, taste and see that the LORD is good!
Blessed is the man who takes refuge in him...
those who seek the LORD lack no good thing."
Psalm 34:8, 10

chapter 9

Paper Clips: This Is Not Going According to Plan

Kaley Rhea

Many are the plans in the mind of a man,
but it is the purpose of the Lord that will stand.
(Proverbs 19:21)

Have you ever tried to pick a lock with a paper clip? According to everything I know from watching TV shows from the 80s, it should take less than five seconds. Under two if you also happen to carry a Swiss Army knife. So when my friends from work were trying to figure out how to unlock a heavy, old metal cabinet no one had a key for, I spoke a very confident game of "You guys. I'm pretty sure I got this."

I broke so many paper clips.

I watched so many YouTube videos.

I scraped a cuticle.

It was a nightmare. Supremely irritating. Nothing about it was going according to plan.

Still in the Planning Stages

Please tell me if I'm the only one: sometimes I get an idea in my head about how my day is going to go. I'm not even a to-do list kind of person or a details kind of person or an itinerary kind of person. Yet somehow I'll have these moments where someone calls or something pops up that throws my preconceived idea of today, of right now, off by a few millimeters, and all my brain alarms go wild and my insides announce loud-speaker style, "Error, error. Please return to regularly scheduled life-having."

To be clear, I am not trying to defend this in any way. This is a ridiculous phenomenon I'm talking about: "I didn't realize the trashcan was full, and now I have to take the trash out, and I wasn't planning on taking the trash out right now. Ugh, worst." And "Oh, my friend is calling, and I love talking to her, but wait, we didn't plan on talking right now; what do I do; why didn't she just text me?" And "Child, why have you vomited on the carpet? We are on our way out the door; I'm not prepared for this!" That moment of internal, irrational pushback I feel when something has intruded into my schedule, into my plans, and something—even something small—is required of me.

Any moment spent remembering that my God knows infinitely more than I do and has made infinitely better plans is a good and necessary moment.

I'm confessing here. Sometimes I live my life with a perspective set about two inches from the end of my nose. I guard my time, my words, my efforts with a sharp eye, unknowingly fixed on only spending them where *I* see fit. And I've met me. So believe me, I know exactly how insane that is.

Back to the Drawing Board

Of course, while ruminating on these things, I thought of Jeremiah 29:11. "'I know the plans I have for you,' says the

LORD. 'Plans for welfare and not for evil. To give you a future and a hope.'" I feel like we pass this verse out like candy, and I'm glad we do because these words are sweet and so important. Any moment spent remembering that my God knows infinitely more than I do and has made infinitely better plans is a good and necessary moment.

But I also couldn't get the Gerasene demoniac out of my mind. Of all the people in the Bible, he's where I landed. Luke 8:26-39 talks about this man who had been possessed by an entire legion of demons and was living an absolutely wrecked life. Jesus cast them out of him. Healed him. So the man made this plan to go with Jesus. It seems like a perfectly legitimate reaction to what had happened. A good, appropriate response. He asked to go, but Jesus told him to stay. To proclaim the name of Jesus where he was. And the man did. Here's the whole thing:

> "Then they sailed to the country of the Gerasenes, which is opposite Galilee. When Jesus had stepped out on land, there met him a man from the city who had demons. For a long time he had worn no clothes, and he had not lived in a house but among the tombs. When he saw Jesus, he cried out and fell down before him and said with a loud voice, "What have you to do with me, Jesus, Son of the Most High God? I beg you, do not torment me." For he had commanded the unclean spirit to come out of the man. (For many a time it had seized him. He was kept under guard and bound with chains and shackles, but he would break the bonds and be driven by the demon into the desert.) Jesus then asked him, "What is your name?" And he said, "Legion," for many demons had entered him. And they begged him not to command them to depart into the abyss. Now a large herd of pigs was feeding there on the hillside,

and they begged him to let them enter these. So he gave them permission. Then the demons came out of the man and entered the pigs, and the herd rushed down the steep bank into the lake and drowned.

"When the herdsmen saw what had happened, they fled and told it in the city and in the country. Then people went out to see what had happened, and they came to Jesus and found the man from whom the demons had gone, sitting at the feet of Jesus, clothed and in his right mind, and they were afraid. And those who had seen it told them how the demon-possessed man had been healed. Then all the people of the surrounding country of the Gerasenes asked him to depart from them, for they were seized with great fear. So he got into the boat and returned. The man from whom the demons had gone begged that he might be with him, but Jesus sent him away, saying, "Return to your home, and declare how much God has done for you." And he went away, proclaiming throughout the whole city how much Jesus had done for him."

A Working Model

It's a convicting thought for me. Jesus has done a miracle in my life, rescued me from the punishment I've earned for myself. And I think sometimes I have this attitude like, "No, no, Jesus, I'm going to serve you this way and in this place and on this timetable," and I miss out on opportunities He lays right in front of me to serve Him and glorify His name. In ways that are simple. In ways that walk right up to me. And instead of thanking Him for these opportunities, in my heart I'm selfishly thinking, "Could you please step aside, Opportunity? I've already scheduled my God-glorifying for 2 p.m., and it's only half past ten now."

I want to be more like this ex-demoniac. He knew exactly what he'd been saved from. He knew he wanted to be close to Jesus. He trusted Jesus enough to let Jesus neatly rearrange his plans. He recognized Jesus as God.

Lord Jesus, wake up my heart. Help me see the things I miss when I focus on my own plans and my own understanding. Holy Spirit, give me kindness. Help me see people the way You see them because I love You. Defeat the selfishness inside of me and replace it with Your love.

"Could you please step aside, Opportunity? I've already scheduled my God-glorifying for 2 p.m., and it's only half past ten now."

Help me hold my plans loosely and always ask You to shape them into whatever You will. I trust You with my time and my desires.

For the record, I never did get that cabinet open. We ended up having it recycled. It could have been full of money and rubies. Or, more probably, the remotes to old VCRs or something.

Sorting It Out

You know who was really ill-prepared and ill-equipped to handle the unexpected curveballs of life? The Gerasene demoniac. You know who Jesus prepared and equipped to handle the unexpected curveballs of life? The Gerasene (formerly known as) demoniac. Jot a few thoughts or prayers to the Lord, asking Him to help you respond with the faith-filled gratefulness of that guy even when you're tempted to see your circumstances more in line with the way those pig farmers did.

_____

_____

_____

Is there anything you've been *begging* Jesus for, like this healed man begged Jesus to let him go with Him? Would you be willing to open up your thinking to include the possibility of His better plan? Talk to Jesus about that.

_____

_____

_____

Would you be willing to pray that wake-up-my-heart kind of prayer every morning? What kind of difference does it make in a person who sincerely asks these kinds of things?

_____

_____

_____

chapter 10

Markers: The God Who Is Bigger Than Your Permanent Marks

Monica Schmelter

Now Thomas, one of the twelve, called the
Twin, was not with them when Jesus came.
So the other disciples told him, "We have
seen the Lord." But he said to them, "Unless
I see in his hands the mark of the nails, and
place my finger into the mark of the nails, and
place my hand into his side, I will never be-
lieve…….. Jesus came and stood among them
and said, "Peace be with you." Then he said
to Thomas, "Put your finger here, and see my
hands; and put out your hand, and place it in
my side. Do not disbelieve, but believe.
(John 20: 24-27)

If you opened the junk drawer in my house you might think that I am a big fan of markers in bright colors. I have markers in neon yellow, orange, green, blue, and hot pink. I don't re-member ever using the markers, but I keep them just in case.

When I was about seven years old, my sister and I decided to play school with markers in our bedroom. My mom said she grew concerned when it got really quiet. As it turns out, her concern was well-founded. My sister and I were writing the ABC's on our bedroom walls with permanent markers.

I won't go into much detail about this incident, but discipline was involved. So was re-painting the room and losing my favorite box of markers for quite a long time.

More Adult Markers

My good friend, Michelle* (I changed her name and a few details to protect privacy and redemption, but the story is true), has experience with markers of the more serious kind. After 16 years of marriage, Michelle's husband wanted a divorce. It was Mother's Day when he initiated the divorce conversation and revealed that he found someone else.

Michelle's husband wasn't forthcoming with details, but he did say how much he loved the other woman. He also added that he hadn't loved Michelle for quite a while. Michelle and her husband had two pre-teen sons and attended church as a family at least 3 times a week.

Michelle's husband was a leader in their church and respected by many. Along with his divorce announcement, he also added that he wasn't so sure about the Christian faith anymore. What?

Michelle was definitely feeling the kind of heartbreak that could mark her life forever. She managed to ask her husband if he would consider counseling. She reminded him how they had both agreed that they would never even use the "D" word. She also mentioned their two boys and the devastation they would experience. Nothing would change his heart or mind. Anger and hurt filled her soul while questions muddled her thinking.

The Other Woman

Who was this other woman? How did they meet? How often did they talk? Did they talk about her? Did the other woman know who she was and what she looked like? With each question Michelle's heart was marked with the excruciating pain of betrayal.

Then Michelle's husband announced a one-week trip to visit his family. He said he wanted to take the boys for a visit with their grandparents. In previous years this had been a family trip. Michelle wondered how and why all of this was happening? Where was God in this?

Michelle's husband ended up dropping the boys off at his parent's house and then taking off for an unnamed destination. He returned to pick the boys up several days later. He brought the boys back to Michelle, packed up his belongings, and moved out.

The "D" Word

Divorce would soon be written in permanent marker on Michelle's heart. Instead of the plan for happily-ever-after, words like *single-mom, co-parenting, divided loyalties,* and *shared holidays* would also be written in permanent marker.

But God would still see Michelle, with no marks.

But God would still see Michelle, with no marks.

In some ways, when Michelle got the initial divorce news, she felt like the female version of the original doubting Thomas. Up until that point, she had followed and trusted Christ without question. Now when faced with the news of the divorce and the other woman, she not only doubted the divorce was real but she wasn't sure what to believe anymore. As Michelle wrestled and prayed over these dark questions, some unusual and amazing changes started to occur.

For example, when her soon-to-be ex-husband made rude comments to her, she didn't retaliate. She returned his insults with kindness and prayer. Prior to the "D" word, Michelle struggled on occasion with fits of rage, anger, jealousy, and gossip. Michelle felt guilty about these episodes, but she accepted them as a part of life in a busy and broken world. Now, the situations that used to trigger Michelle's anger seemed inconsequential.

Riddled with Doubt

Her opinions on the man some call doubting Thomas were changing too.

For years, she thought of Thomas as a marginal believer who had to be scolded by Jesus because of his doubts. Now Michelle reasons that Jesus met Thomas at his place of need. Perhaps it wasn't so much a scolding as it was Jesus making a special effort to reassure Thomas that his faith was not in vain.

You just can't overlook the lengths to which Jesus went to reassure a man riddled with doubt.

Of course, there is also the part of the conversation where Jesus says we are blessed when we don't see and still believe. Even in light of that exchange, you just can't overlook the lengths to which Jesus went to reassure a man riddled with doubt.

The Marks to Prove It

When Jesus appeared to the fearful disciples after the resurrection, He spoke peace to them first. Before their conversation went any further, He wanted their hearts to be still. In the middle of their chaotic world, He says the same to us today: "Peace I leave with you; my peace I give to you. Not as the world gives do I give to you. Let not your hearts be troubled, neither let them be afraid" (John 14:27).

After quieting their hearts, He showed them His nail-marked hands and pierced side. He allowed them to see that He was the Resurrected Christ. He even had the marks to prove it.

Before Jesus' death, the marks touted the plan of the evil one. After His resurrection, the marks and every force of hell were disarmed. "He disarmed the rulers and authorities and put them to open shame, by triumphing over them in him" (Colossians 2:15).

What if we dared to believe that we could walk in Resurrection power and that even our marks must yield to God's plan for our lives? "The Spirit of God, who raised Jesus from the dead, lives in you. And just as God raised Christ Jesus from the dead, he will give life to your mortal bodies by this same Spirit living within you" (Romans 8:11, NLT).

We are made whole as we rely on His truth. As Michelle relied on His resurrection power within her, she began to see that she could walk in victory despite her painful divorce. She stopped thinking about herself as a vulnerable single mom, betrayed woman, and hot mess. By faith Michelle started allowing Christ's power to override the fallout of her failed marriage.

Marker of Betrayal

The same is true for you and me. Whether it is rejection, divorce, betrayal, anxiety, trauma, drama, depression, bankruptcy or any other attack that can leave us marked up, it does not have to derail God's good plan for our lives. While our faith in Christ doesn't make our marks disappear, it does gives us a framework of truth from which to build. For Michelle, this means that the marker of betrayal succumbs to God's restoration power. Over time and by faith, Michelle began to believe that even her most painful markers could yield to God's good plan for her life.

As Michelle dared to see her life through Christ's victory on the cross, she was able to move forward with hope for her future. She was also able to forgive her ex-husband and the other woman by opening her heart to God's healing and restoration in her life. The pain that had marked her life began to give way to God's power to overcome and live in freedom.

Twinge of Regret

Michelle and the boys are doing very well now. They moved to a new community and are a part of a great church family. Michelle has a job she mostly likes and enjoys trying new adventures like rock climbing and Thai food.

That's not to say she never has a bad day or feels a twinge of regret over what might have been. But the mark is superseded by God's unfailing love.

Michelle's ex and his new wife are doing well too. They are all co-parenting the boys and working together for the good of their future. Before we get angry that Michelle's ex and the other woman are doing well, we need to remember that God is good. We should never mistake His grace for affirming bad behavior. Michelle knows and rests in that.

Even though I love the colors of the markers in my junk drawer, I rarely if ever use them. I have plenty of experience though with adult-sized markers that, without God's intervention, spell failure and disaster. The solution is never as easy as repainting a room, but God is always faithful. When we dare to believe His Word, even our markers yield to God's good plan for our lives.

Sorting It Out

Identify your Markers	Now See Your Marker Through Christ's Power

chapter 11

String: Untangling Our Discontentment

Rhonda Rhea

I have learned in whatever situation I
am to be content.
(Philippians 4:11)

I try not to keep much string in my junk drawer. Not because I don't like string or because I don't need string. But it's more because if there's a string to be seen, there's something eerily peculiar inside me that makes me want to pull it. I'm not content to simply let it dangle there. Must. Pull. What kind of weird string compulsion is this?

That means you should be warned. That sweater in your closet? The sweater that's notorious for stray threads? If there's a chance I'll be wherever you're headed, don't wear it. I'll try not to pull that little string. But let's face it, I'm going to pull that string. It's not even all that satisfying for me. But I'm pulling it. I wonder if there's a word for this specific lunacy. String-o-mania?

Am I Just Stringing Words Together?

Did you know there's a word for just about every compulsion? Pteridomania is a passion for ferns. Choreomania?

A dancing frenzy. Clininomania is an excessive desire to stay in bed. That one did make me yawn—but it was just a small yawn.

There are more. And before you ask, let me go ahead and tell you that I'm not making these up. Sophomania is the delusion that a person is extraordinarily intelligent. I'm smart enough to know I don't have that one. If you are a doromaniac, you are obsessed with giving gifts...and I would like to be your friend. I would list a bunch more here, but an excessive compulsion to accumulate facts is called "infomania," so I'm not going there.

Just one more: verbomania. Another real one. It's defined as a "craze for words." Oh wow, I'm not at all happy to tell you that my manias do seem to be piling up. I think on top of verbomania, I likely also have nounomania (no, it's not a real thing). Adjectivomania, too (also not a thing). Every once in a while, I'll slip in some adverbomania (still not a thing). Seems to me, though, if I want complete sentences, I'm going to need the entire complement of the word-disorders.

Stringing Along the Dissatisfaction

Some people seem to have a natural, comfortable way with words. They effortlessly string them together, as it were, with hardly a thought. Words, sentences, paragraphs—they all just flow out of those people, all polished and pretty. The fact that I don't despise those people is a testament to how truly spiritual I am. (If you're not rolling your eyes right here, then you're obviously even more spiritual than I am.)

Most of the time my words have to be coaxed, wheedled, and prodded. My muse cops an attitude and is all like, "Not today, suckah." Then when I finally do get some words down, I still have to edit them up one side and down the other.

Writers of my caliber? We're the ones who want the words—written or spoken—all perfectly packaged. And we're constantly stepping back to look at the package, thinking things like, "That package really could've used a bigger bow.

Maybe a red one. Perhaps an entirely different paper. Also... let's just make it a different package altogether." Incidentally, we're the same people who spend a good minute and a half practicing to get the wording exactly right in our heads before ordering into the drive-through speaker. Taco-Bell-o-phobia?

For Want of a Better Word

Word-discontent. I have it often. As a matter of fact, I just edited those last few sentences, like, six times. Then still left word-discontent and Taco-Bell-o-phobia in there, pretending they're grammatically sound. And pretending they're actually words.

Discontentment is a tricky rascal. All kinds of discontentment originate in the thinking we need something different than we have. Something better. Something in a different package. Something with a red bow. Something more. And at every level of discontentment is that next little niggling thought that we will never be truly happy until we have that something more.

That kind of dissatisfaction always breeds conflict—within ourselves and with other people as well. "What is the source of wars and fights among you? Don't they come from the cravings that are at war within you?" (James 4:1, HCSB).

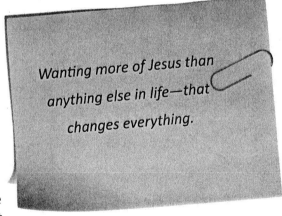

Wanting more of Jesus than anything else in life—that changes everything.

A Word on a Better "Want"

Are you warring with dissatisfaction and all the wrong wants—maybe even warring with others because of it? Want to change that? There's only one way to stop wanting more. And that is to want a different kind of more. More Jesus.

Wanting more of Jesus than anything else in life—that changes everything. Focusing on Him shines a light on any selfish wants and they're seen for the empty, unfulfilling distractions they really are.

Wanting more Jesus is a life pursuit. Maybe not so much coaxing, wheedling, and prodding, but it is learned, day by day, and it requires our attention. As we give that attention to times of seeking the Lord's face in prayer, making His Word part of our everyday life and our everyday thinking, and letting those connections with Him make us quick to get rid of sin, we find the temporary things of this world less appealing. And we find His love, His truth, His "Him-ness," so much more desirous than anything else we've ever known. (Yes, I just wrote the word, "Him-ness" in there—with nary an eye-roll.)

At that place of praise-filled closeness to Him we're drawn into worship. It's impossible to worship in His fullness and still want what we're not supposed to want. In worship we're reminded we truly do have everything we need. In Ephesians 1:3, Paul praises the Father who "has blessed us in Christ with every spiritual blessing."

Discontentment? Bye-bye. Because...not today, suckah!

Wait, did I word that wrong?

Sorting It Out

If you're in a battle with discontentment, could I challenge you to sort through some of your thinking? Instead of brooding about the couldas of life, or maybe even the shouldas, and instead of wanting, wishing, and regretting your energies away, how about determining to find your contentment in the one place where it's stable and satisfying. It's only in the Lord, in trusting Him, depending on Him, worshipping Him, allowing Him to sort out our should-have-beens and remind us that He's the one who will accomplish everything that counts. We can line up our thinking with His through meditating on His Word. Let's start with the words of Jesus in Matthew 6:30-34:

> "'But if God so clothes the grass of the field, which today is alive and tomorrow is thrown into the oven, will he not much more clothe you, O you of little faith? Therefore do not be anxious, saying, 'What shall we eat?' or 'What shall we drink?' or 'What shall we wear?' For the Gentiles seek after all these things, and your heavenly Father knows that you need them all. But seek first the kingdom of God and his righteousness, and all these things will be added to you. Therefore do not be anxious about tomorrow, for tomorrow will be anxious for itself. Sufficient for the day is its own trouble.'"

Does this passage inspire a prayer? Write it out to your Father:

_____

_____

_____

_____

_____

_____

How about a little added input and an additional perspective on the Matthew 6 passage from a paraphrase? Read it again in *The Message,* underlining the sections that inspire you, then write out your additional thoughts and insights. Ask Him to lead you to focus on Him—and to show you exactly how true it is that "your everyday human concerns will be met."

> "If God gives such attention to the appearance of wildflowers—most of which are never even seen—don't you think he'll attend to you, take

pride in you, do his best for you? What I'm trying to do here is to get you to relax, to not be so preoccupied with *getting,* so you can respond to God's *giving.* People who don't know God and the way he works fuss over these things, but you know both God and how he works. Steep your life in God-reality, God-initiative, God-provisions. Don't worry about missing out. You'll find all your everyday human concerns will be met. Give your entire attention to what God is doing right now, and don't get worked up about what may or may not happen tomorrow. God will help you deal with whatever hard things come up when the time comes" (Matthew 6:30-34, The Message).

_____
_____
_____
_____
_____
_____

"You keep him in perfect peace whose mind is stayed on you, because he trusts in you. Trust in the LORD forever, for the LORD GOD is an everlasting rock" (Isaiah 26:3-4).

chapter 12

Razors: Stay Sharp!

Kaley Rhea

*For the word of God is living
and active, sharper than any two-edged
sword, piercing to the division of soul and of
spirit, of joints and of marrow, and discerning
the thoughts and intentions of the heart.*
(Hebrews 4:12)

You know how a lot of times you'll have your deepest, most philosophically significant thoughts in the solitude of the shower or bathtub? Allow me to share an example of...not that.

The other night I was tired. Not exhausted. Just normal mid-week fatigue that crops up every so often. Decided to take a bath. Because that sounds like pure heaven for a tired person. My tired brain was, I suppose, off doing its own thing, and I nicked my knee while shaving my legs. Little bit of blood, no big deal; you know the drill.

In that moment, the thought that formed in my mind while watching that little bit of blood in the water was *Uh, oh.*

I better watch out for sharks.

Yes, go ahead and read that thought again slowly. It's fine.

Because I worried about sharks. While sitting in my bathtub.

If I could just take a moment here: I live in Missouri. Probably the most landlocked state in the United States. If TV and books and the internet weren't around, I would not know an animal called a shark exists. And none of that's even relevant actually because sharks do not happen in bathtubs. At least not by accident. Certainly not without being extremely conspicuous! Brain, what were you doing?

Sharps Attack

Later, after the bath (because again, this is not a story of deep shower thoughts), it hit me how my mind is so programmed to worry. I can worry in my sleep. Without breaking a sweat—without even noticing—I can worry about things that are irrelevant, implausible, or imaginary. That is where my mind, in its natural state, wants to live.

That is not a happy place to live. There are sharks there apparently.

Philippians 4 verse 6 reads, "do not be anxious about anything, but in everything by prayer and supplication with thanksgiving let your requests be made known to God." I hear and see this verse quoted a lot. Maybe you do, too, and you're like me and think *Okay, easier said than done, Paul, thanks.* But have you noticed this verse connects to verse 5? It's always a good idea to read the verse or two surrounding the ones you're studying because it can give you some beautiful context like this. Just before "do not be anxious," it says simply, "The Lord is at hand."

"The Lord is at hand; do not be anxious..." Let me tell you, something, friend. If I am at hand, you need to be anxious. If you are at hand, worry is the completely correct response. But the Lord is at hand. Jesus Christ, the Word of God who became flesh, the One through whom everything that is made has been made, the defeater of death, our champion, risen from the grave—He is at hand. Don't worry.

Furthermore, and I love this, when the Lord is at hand, instead of worrying, I can pray. When the Lord is at hand, I can check my arrogance at the door. When the Lord is at hand, I can be thankful.

I have a brain built here in a fallen world. It will tell me the appropriate response to every cut and scrape is to worry about sharks. And you know what? Sometimes there really are sharks out there. Our world is not made of friendly plushes and flouncy pillows. There are sharp teeth and jagged edges and hard things that cut.

But how wonderful to know my Lord knows this. He knit my brain together. And in His incomprehensible kindness, He's already told me what to do when I feel worried. I don't know about you, but that makes me feel so loved. Cause I am. So are you.

> *Our world is not made of friendly plushes and flouncy pillows. There are sharp teeth and jagged edges and hard things that cut. But how wonderful to know my Lord knows this.*

Philippians 4 continues with verse 7: "And the peace of God, which surpasses all understanding, will guard your hearts and your minds in Christ Jesus."

Lord Jesus, thank You so much for being everything I need. For being bigger than my darkest fears and for loving me enough to allow me to draw close to You and figure out my feelings when I'm anxious. When I am tempted to give in to worry, renew my mind, Lord, by Your Spirit, and set it on You. I know worrying about all the sharp things of life does not make me sharper.

It dulls me, wearies me, leaves me feeling unprepared and vulnerable. Please sharpen me by Your Word, by Your presence, by Your goodness, and by Your power. Help my heart remember how to be thankful. In Jesus's mighty name.

Sorting It Out

What's your greatest fear or worry?

_____

_____

_____

_____

I want to share this with you: In John chapter 11, Jesus' good friend Lazarus became sick and eventually died. Jesus told his disciples they were about to go back to Judea, and they rightly reminded Him He nearly got murdered last time they were there. Jesus said some things they didn't understand and then translated it into, "Lazarus has died...Let us go to him (v. 14-15)."

They did go with him, and Jesus—by His plan and in His time—did an unthinkable miracle when He brought a man four days dead back to life.

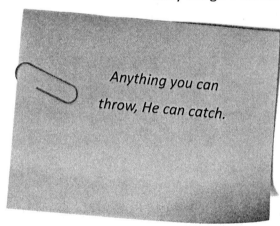

Anything you can throw, He can catch.

But I want to talk about Thomas the Apostle here. Look at John 11:16 with me.

"So Thomas, called the Twin, said to his fellow disciples, 'Let us also go, that we may die with him.'"

I love that. So much. Because this is the same guy every-one knows as Doubting Thomas. And at a glance, it seems like what he's doing in this passage is flipping his dyed-black bangs out of his eyes, pulling his hood up over his head, and saying, "Well, Jesus is being unreasonable again; so I guess let's all go die." Like leave it to Doubting Fluffy-Dark-Raincloud-of-Doom Thomas to put the "fatal" in fatalistic, right? But I don't think that's what he did at all.

You see, I want brave Thomas's answer to be my answer. When the Lord through His Word or His Spirit asks me to do something I don't understand. That may require a sacrifice. That frightens me. Even if what He's asking me to do is to let Him replace my worries with trust in Him.

Death is the scariest thing I can think of, and Jesus already took care of that for me. Proved He is stronger. Proved He loves me enough, even while I'm undeserving. And He is more than capable of taking care of:

Death of my comfort.
Death of my pride.
Death of an unhealthy relationship.
Death of my expectations.
Death of my need to feel in control.

I want to be willing to say to my Father, with my Raincloud of Doom hood swept back from my face, "Whatever the cost, I want to go with You."

Is there something in your life you're struggling to hold on to? Something you're unwilling to surrender? Maybe it's not something you've identified as a fear, but something you've decided you're better suited to harbor than the Lord is.

_____

_____

_____

Take a few moments with the Lord. Tell Him. Tell Him your fears. Tell Him your reasons. Cast your cares, and ask Him to carry them. He can take it, I promise. He is strong enough. He is loving enough. Anything you can throw, He can catch.

chapter 13

Remote Controls and Social Media: Electronic Time-outs

Monica Schmelter

Soon afterward he went on through cities and villages, proclaiming and bringing the good news of the kingdom of God. And the twelve were with him, and also some women who had been healed of evil spirits and infirmities: Mary, called Magdalene, from whom seven demons had gone out, and Joanna, the wife of Chuza, Herod's household manager, and Susanna, and many others, who provided for them out of their means.
(Luke 8:1-4)

There are many brave women in the Bible who risked everything to follow Jesus. A few of them are named in first few verses in chapter 8 of Luke. They are Mary Magdalene, Joanna, and Susanna. The most recognized name in that list is Mary Magdalene. She is frequently referred to as the woman who was healed of seven demons. While her demonic deliverance is a miracle of monumental proportions, that is only the starting place when it comes to learning from her life and faith.

Mary Magdalene courageously followed Jesus at a point in history when women were widely regarded as second-class citizens. Even without premier social status, Mary Magdalene accumulated resources and freely shared them to support the work of Christ. Her tenacity started there and followed her all the way to the cross and the empty tomb.

Unafraid to be Counted

While Jesus hung on the cross, she stood by bravely, apparently unafraid to be counted as one of His followers. Even after his death she wanted to help prepare His body for burial. These acts of faith were greatly rewarded as she was the first person to hear the words of our risen Savior, Jesus Christ.

> "But Mary stood weeping outside the tomb, and as she wept she stooped to look into the tomb. And she saw two angels in white, sitting where the body of Jesus had lain, one at the head and one at the feet. They said to her, 'Woman, why are you weeping?' She said to them, 'They have taken away my Lord, and I do not know where they have laid him.' Having said this, she turned around and saw Jesus standing, but she did not know that it was Jesus. Jesus said to her, 'Woman, why are you weeping? Whom are you seeking?' Supposing him to be the gardener, she said to him, 'Sir, if you have carried him away, tell me where you have laid him, and I will take him away.'
> "Jesus said to her, 'Mary.' She turned and said to him in Aramaic 'Rabboni!' (which means Teacher). Jesus said to her, 'Do not cling to me,

for I have not yet ascended to the Father; but go to my brothers and say to them, "I am ascending to my Father and your Father, to my God and your God."' Mary Magdalene went and announced to the disciples, 'I have seen the Lord'—and that he had said these things to her" (John 20:11-18).

Imagine her joy to see our Savior and hear His first words after the resurrection. All of her tenacity, faith, bravery, and financial sacrifices are richly rewarded in this one conversation.

The Bible doesn't record a lot of details about Mary Magdalene's daily schedule and routine. What we do know, based on her bravery and level of sacrifice, was that her relationship with Jesus Christ was her foremost priority. She would have never been able to follow Him so consistently or in the face of such adversity, without daily time in His presence and obedience to His Word.

It can be easy enough for those of us engaged in this modern world to look back at Mary Magdalene and all the others and conclude that it was probably easier to follow Christ in that time period. After all, they didn't have the distractions of modern-day technology. They didn't have cell phones, televisions, remote controls, or any of the techno gadgets available in today's marketplace. But their lives were at risk.

Nothing Worth Watching

They didn't do DVR programming or replace batteries in remote controls. They never faced the dilemma of

Certainly, modern-day technology was not a part of the landscape in biblical times, but distractions have always been an option in a fallen world.

what to watch on television. Nor did they experience the silliness of scanning through a hundred channels in seconds flat only to discover there was nothing worth watching. Certainly, modern-day technology was not a part of the landscape in biblical times, but distractions have always been an option in a fallen world.

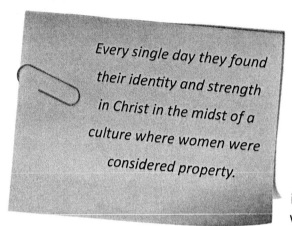

Every single day they found their identity and strength in Christ in the midst of a culture where women were considered property.

Mary Magdalene, Joanna, Susanna, and the other women who courageously followed Jesus had to choose to follow Him every day. Every single day they found their identity and strength in Christ in the midst of a culture where women were considered property.

They also lavishly worshiped Jesus in the middle of a religious system that didn't recognize women. While these cultural truths would take the wind out of most people's sails, these women continued on and even gave of their own resources to support the work of Christ. Why? What would make these women do that? Even in biblical times there had to be other ways for them to spend their time and money.

Love

They chose Jesus over everyone and everything else in the world every single day because they knew what really mattered. They knew He loved them. They knew that Jesus was their ultimate reward. They knew that long after all was said and done, Jesus was their only hope and truest reward, so they lived for Him every single day despite the cost.

We can do that too. Sure, it takes some planning and sacrifice. But then it becomes second nature. In a world in love with devices, it means we turn off screens every once in a while. Sometimes a device-free zone is what we need to rest, recharge and clearly hear from Him.

Losing the Remote Control

Sometimes the best sanity retention moments come from losing the remote control on purpose to read His Word. In His Word, we find Jesus, the lover of our soul and author and finisher of our faith. In His Word, we find His plan for our lives, along with courage for our daily decisions.

The women we find in Luke chapter 8 faced different distractions than we do today. While they didn't have the temptation to check their social media accounts every 2.5 seconds, they still needed the same tenacious faith to make Christ their first priority. So the question becomes, how? How do we make the brave choices that ensure Christ is our primary concern? How do we manage in a world filled with devices and still find regular quiet time in His presence? While I don't have all the answers, I do know that having a plan is essential. The plan needs to include consistent time to rest, recover, and experience renewal.

For my friend Barbara, every Sunday is a device-free day. That's right, her cell phone, remote control, and laptop remain in the off position for a full 24 hours. Sundays are her day to read, pray, enjoy church, and fellowship. Barbara says going device-free was awful at first. Then Sundays gradually became a place of rest that brought her much needed peace and clarity. For me, it means the cell phone goes into "Do Not Disturb" mode every evening at 8 PM. Facebook notifications and the remote control go in the off position as I open my heart to worshiping the Lord and reading His Word. For another it means phones in priority mode letting through only the emergency calls of your aging parents or your partying teens.

Benefits of Consistent Rest

Your device-free zone may look different as well. What's important is that you receive the benefits of consistent rest and recovery so that you can be renewed. I look forward to this special time, as it is truly my haven from an overwhelming world filled with technology that is both wonderful and maddening.

Take some time to find what works for you. I've learned that God doesn't always give an immediate download of four easy steps to follow each and every day. Many times it starts with a thought like, "Maybe I should try putting my phone in Do Not Disturb each evening at 8 PM to take time to worship and read." Of course, as I start to do what I think the Lord might wanting me to do, I also start to second guess myself. This may be prompted by fear of missing a call or desire to watch a particular program. Or maybe I fall asleep at 8 PM, so the time needs to be 7 PM. What I am saying is that sometimes your plan for a device-free zone may take a little time to unfold. Just start with what you know and stick with what works for you.

Just as Jesus had to go away to a lonely place to seek His Father, we do too. The more we seek Him the more we find Him. That doesn't mean we only talk to Him during those times. We also talk to him while sitting at family suppers, asking for just the words to encourage the fourth grader who hasn't found this year's friends. But it does mean we find some time for just God and me.

> "Ask, and it will be given to you; seek, and you will find; knock, and it will be opened to you" (Matthew 7:7).

> "And without faith it is impossible to please him, for whoever would draw near to God must believe that he exists and that he rewards those who seek him" (Hebrews 11:6).

Sorting it Out

Do you struggle with a regular quiet time with God? If so, how can you start to change that?

_____

_____

_____

What is something you would really like to change about your quiet time with God?

_____

_____

_____

What if you approached your device-free zone by considering the benefits of rest, recovery, and renewal? How might that change things?

_____

_____

_____

chapter 14

Dead Batteries: The Power to Rejoice

Rhonda Rhea

Friends, when life gets really difficult, don't
jump to the conclusion that God isn't on the
job. Instead, be glad that you are in the very
thick of what Christ experienced. This is a
spiritual refining process, with glory
just around the corner.
(1 Peter 4:12-13 The Message)

All these dead batteries in this drawer. What is it that makes a person stick a dead battery back in a drawer? And why are the dead ones all mixed in with the good ones?

My uncle always said the only way to tell for sure if it's a good battery or not is to stick your tongue on it. If your ears don't ring for a half hour, you should throw it away. My hair was curlier when I was a kid and I think this may be why.

There were a lot of frizzy-haired battery searches when I was little. Probably even more of those searches as I was raising my own kids. How many batteries does it take, for instance, to power the average American post-Christmas playtime? If I were to make a joke out of that question, it would probably include a clever play on words—maybe something about lithium ion versus lead oxide. No doubt we'd all get a big charge out of it. (A "charge"? Really? That's all I could come up with there?)

Charging Ahead

I'm confessing here that at my house we continue to buy batteries by the boatload around Christmastime—even now that my kids are grown. Most of the batteries are for my husband. He still gets toys for Christmas. I would tease him about that except that I buy him most of the toys. And also I like toys.

I'm not sure I can even count the number of batteries we drained the year Richie got the remote-controlled helicopter. One of my favorite incidents that year was when he was still trying to learn how to fly it. Where's an anti-torque pedal when you need one? He accidentally landed it right smack-dab in a big bowl of strawberry preserves. Unexpected. And so funny! And hey, new invention: *jelly-copter.*

A friend pointed out that all he needs to do now is learn how to land in the peanut butter. Then he'll be able to make a sandwich without ever getting out of his chair. Mmmm. Peanut butter and choppers.

Remote Control, Out of Control

On the other hand, it's not nearly so funny when life is feeling out of control, and we find ourselves landing in something sticky. But we're told in 1 Peter 4:12 that it shouldn't be so unexpected. "Beloved, do not be surprised at the fiery trial when it comes upon you to test you, as though something strange were happening to you."

Wouldn't it be nice if we never experienced those out-of-control-feeling moments—if we didn't have to struggle through the sticky? Our someday will be without difficult surprises. But in our here and now, living in a sin-cursed world makes a fiery ordeal a very common part of the journey.

We have a tendency to think our suffering is unique. But for the most part, it's not. Peter's "do not be surprised" is in the present imperative form—a command. The command is to stop it. Stop thinking this is unusual. We have to chose to stop. Sometimes when we've been closely following Christ, our inclination is to be offended by a trial—to wonder "what did I do to deserve *this*?"

Our God Is Still "In Charge"

One paraphrase puts it this way: "Friends, when life gets really difficult, don't jump to the conclusion that God isn't on the job" (The Message)..

In those moments when life is the stickiest, we can look at the difficulty as some kind of punishment or crushing defeat—even the absence of God working (which many people do), or we can see it for what it really is. It's the result of living in a fallen world. Sometimes it's also a part of a refining process the Lord wants to use to conform us to the image of Christ.

We have instructions in just how we should respond in the very next verse. "But rejoice insofar as you share Christ's sufferings, that you may also rejoice and be glad when his glory is revealed" (1 Peter 4:13).

As the Holy Spirit works in us, we truly can find ourselves rejoicing, all by His limitless power—even in the stickiest trials. Next thing you know, you have a glorious testimony—maybe enough to fill a book!

Booking Our Next Adventure

You can probably guess that I love books.

When life is the stickiest, we can look at the difficulty as some kind of punishment or crushing defeat—even the absence of God working, or we can see it for what it really is.

Reading them, writing them. Both are an adventure. Especially reading the adventure-y books.

Those adventure books, the really intense kind? I love them. And I hate them. And I love to hate them. About the entire aim of writing in most suspense is getting readers to love a character—and then tormenting that character within an inch of his imaginary life with near-unbearable problems, danger, stress, and anguish. Before you can recover, the writer tosses in another devastating struggle. And a heartbreak. Probably as he's hanging from a cliff. Maybe then a natural disaster on top of that. Possibly two.

I'm always trying to prepare myself for the nail-biting agony of that hopeless moment—the one when your favorite character is trapped with no shred of hope for rescue or escape. He almost always does escape, of course. But by then I pretty much need a shower. Sometimes a nap.

As a writer, I want to write stories that deliver readers the same kind of compelling need to stop reading because the story is just too intense. And to keep reading because the story is just too intense. Not that we writers are insecure or anything, but every once in a while, my inner critic tells me that I am to writing as Spam is to meat. Hush up, inner critic. I love writing. And I hate it. And I love hating it.

Love/Hate and Hate/Hate

While it may be a love/hate relationship with suspense and writing, in real life I'm much more inclined to think of intense struggles as more of a hate/hate thing. I don't think I'm alone there. Difficulties in relationships, challenging circumstances, cruel people, financial problems, health issues—sometimes they're the kind of struggles that leave a person feeling trapped with no hope of rescue. Just too intense.

Still, it's in those intense times that we do well to consider that our rescue or escape physically is not nearly as imperative as it is spiritually. What a great ending to our story: the spiritual is perfectly settled in the most happily-ever-after kind of way.

Paul tells us that our God "has rescued us from the domain of darkness and transferred us into the kingdom of the Son He loves. We have redemption, the forgiveness of sins, in Him," (Colossians 1:13-14 HCSB). Rescued! Forever freed! Now there's some beautiful drama.

The two verses right before that passage give us an important how-to when it comes to dealing with the struggles of this life. "May you be strengthened with all power, according to His glorious might, for all endurance and patience, with joy giving thanks to the Father, who has enabled you to share in the saints' inheritance in the light" (vv. 11-12, HCSB).

Powering UP, Powering IN

The power we need for overcoming the obstacles of life? That strength and power comes from the God who indwells us! The strength to endure, to have patience, to solve the situation, to find joy, to be thankful—He will empower us for all of that from the inside out, no matter how steep the cliff we're hanging from.

It's good to ask our Father to rescue us physically. We see it all through the Bible—you can pick almost any Psalm. But regardless of the hows and whens of His answers, we can rest assured there is never a hopeless moment for us. This, I love to love. The walk of faith is all wrapped up in hope. We're wrapped. Not trapped.

We can find perfect rest in that hope. That's better than any nap. And it comes with our magnificent charge to trust, rest in the Lord, and trust some more.

For this charge? Batteries not included. Or needed.

Sorting It Out:

Take a look at the passage in 1 Peter in the Amplified Version:

> "Beloved, do not be surprised at the fiery ordeal which is taking place to test you [that is,

to test the quality of your faith], as though something strange *or* unusual were happening to you. But insofar as you are sharing Christ's sufferings, keep on rejoicing, so that when His glory [filled with His radiance and splendor] is revealed, you may rejoice with great joy" (1 Peter 4:12-13 AMP).

In your struggle or test of the moment, how might God be charging you to "keep on rejoicing"?

_____

_____

_____

If you have found yourself thinking you're alone in your suffering and that your difficulty is unique, how can you obey the command to stop being surprised? Is there anything that needs to change in your thinking about trials? If so, what—and what steps can you take to renew your thinking?

_____

_____

_____

Make a list of the lovely rejoice-ables in your life right now.

_____

_____

_____

How can this list—and thoughts of the God who is worthy of your trust—restore your faith and charge up your hope through the temporary difficulties of this life?

_____

_____

_____

chapter 15

Mints: Need to Refresh?
It's How We're "Mint" to Live

Kaley Rhea

Unless the Lord builds the house, those who build it labor in vain. Unless the Lord watches over the city, the watchman stays awake in vain. It is in vain that you rise up early and go late to rest, eating the bread of anxious toil; for he gives to his beloved sleep.
(Psalm 127:1-2)

Let's talk about rest, kids!

I want to start by giving a nod to a champion rester. My pup, Lu Lu Rhea. She is a ten-pound Pekingese mixed with poodle mixed with Chihuahua mixed with a loaf of stale white bread. And even if it seems like she could use one of the eight thousand breath mints from my junk drawer, I have to give her props on the fact she is never happier than when she is resting on one of her humans. I normally don't want to be anything like Lu. Because too often she's ripping a paper plate to shreds or making whimpering demands for lunch meat. But there is one page I wouldn't mind taking from her book. Or, more to the point, from God's book.

We all know the busyness. The demands. The constant stream of input. There are loads of studies out there reporting in about all the ways we're wired to need rest. Google it; it's fascinating. As far as I can tell, there is no rogue faction of the scientific community pushing the idea that rest is not absolutely essential to our ability to function. In fact, the more research done on the subject the more apparent it becomes. Mind, body, soul, they're all knit together. They all affect each other; and as much as they require challenges and exercising and work, they all require rest.

But sometimes I think there is so much depending on me. That if I stop, if I readjust, if I rest, then something I'm holding up with my own strength will fall. When the truth is, anything I'm holding up with my own strength will fall regardless. All rest does is help me see Who really holds all things together.

Sugar Free. Sweetened with Jesus Extract.

Personally, I adore this moment in Mark 6:30-32 where "The apostles returned to Jesus and told him all that they had done and taught. And he said to them, 'Come away by yourselves to a desolate place and rest a while.' For many were coming and going, and they had no leisure even to eat. And they went away in the boat to a desolate place by themselves." It's super sweet to me picturing Jesus shepherding these boys along like "Good job, please have a sandwich."

Getting alone with the Lord, while making sure my physical needs are met so I can think straight while I spend time with Him, makes a huge difference in my life. The introvert part of me loves the desolate place bit, I won't lie. As much as I love people, sometimes I just need Jesus, a sandwich, and a desolate place. Not forever. But for a while.

Let's read Exodus 34:21. "Six days you shall work, but on the seventh day you shall rest. In plowing time and in harvest you shall rest."

It's very interesting to me that it doesn't say, "When plowing time is over you shall rest." It doesn't say, "After you've had a successful harvest you shall rest."

Yes, we are to work. Of course, we are to work. God places callings on our lives, purposes us, equips us to get stuff done. But even during those busy seasons, when our minds and maybe even our peers or our friends or our families seem to want to convince us that taking a day or even an hour for rest is an offense, selfish, and thoughtless in nature, please disregard. Please encourage your mind and your peer/friend/family member to take a break. You don't work better if you haven't gotten a rest. You work worse. And you feel worse. When I depend on me instead of on God's grace, I always feel worse.

Please don't hear me being legalistic about this. Don't hear me putting more on your plate. Don't hear me accusing or whining or saying any version of "Some of you have been doing this all wrong." I hope for you this is freeing. My hope is there are burdens lifted here. I want to revel in this with you. I want to praise God in this

> Yes, we are to work. Of course, we are to work. God places callings on our lives, purposes us, equips us to get stuff done.

with you. This is Jesus Christ, creative power of holy, righteous, mighty God, essentially saying to his bride, "Babe, I got this. Why don't you go lay down for a bit." Does that not make you melt with affection for Him?

Life Savers

I've never hesitated to do a trust fall. Ever. But I'll admit it's less because I'm a trusting person and more because I'm short enough that a fall from this height wouldn't cause any real damage.

But in 7th grade I went to a cheerleading practice. Suddenly they wanted me to let my fellow twelve- and thirteen-year-old girls lift me up, throw me into the air, and catch me. Have you ever heard the sound of twelve- or thirteen-year-olds catching another twelve- or thirteen-year-old out of the air? I will tell you. It sounds like getting punched in the face. Oh, I nope-d right outta there. Hard. Really put my trust fall record into perspective.

I think I tend to do the same thing with the Lord. Father, I will trust you only as far as I can be sure I won't get hurt. Or only as far as I have a backup plan in place. Or only as far as I'm really the one in control here. Which is no kind of trust at all.

Breathe Out

In my life I have determined—through a great deal of data analysis and scientific observations—there are three specific situations during which I most need reminding that God is the One in control:

1. When everything feels out of control.
2. When I've accidentally convinced myself I am in control.
3. All the other times.

It is so easy when things go wrong to lose sight of the One we can absolutely trust. Or maybe even to look at God—who is in control, after all—and to blame Him. *How could He let this happen? Why didn't He stop this? Do you see now why I can't close my eyes, God?*

I don't know the answer every time to be honest. What I do know every time is that God is good. He is the source of goodness. What I do know every time is God loves you and me. He is the God who loved us enough to send his Son Jesus to die where we deserved to die.

God is good, even in a fallen world. God is love, even when it seems like your fallen world is especially falling apart. When you are hurting, devastated, max-level stressed, or even just proud, and you wonder *Can I trust God? Can I really trust Him?* While you're quoting Jeremiah 29:11 to yourself, maybe listen to Paul in Romans 8, too, where he writes, "For I am convinced that neither death nor life, neither angels nor demons, neither the present nor the future, nor any powers, neither height nor depth, nor anything else in all creation, will be able to separate us from the love of God that is in Christ Jesus our Lord (vs. 38-39 NIV)."

Paul, whose life was filled with more hardship than I know how to imagine, had this brilliant, God-given trust that none of those hardships for one moment could keep him from experiencing the love God had for him. He could feel secure in God's love in the face of everything. He had that assurance because of Jesus. When his body hurt and his stomach was empty and his life was in danger, he could rest.

So I suppose in my life I have discovered—only through a miracle of grace—there are three specific things I need when I am arrogant or weary or battered enough to forget in Whom I can find my rest:

1. I need to focus on Jesus.
2. I need to read about Jesus.
3. I need to ask Jesus to, by His grace, give me the wisdom to show me what to do when everything human in me is screaming *Jesus may be the answer to a lot of things, but Jesus can't be the answer to this.*

Jesus is the answer to this. If Jesus is the answer in the face of death and demons and "anything else in all creation," Jesus is the answer to every one of your this-es.

Through every season, I want to encourage and remind my soul to find the kind of delight resting close to my Master that Lu Lu Rhea, the princess of all puppers, finds in resting close to hers. Also I'm taking recommendations on good doggy breath-fresheners. If you know any.

> *Dear Jesus,*
> *You are perfect. You love me perfectly. Remind me through your Spirit there is no height I could fall from too high for You to catch me. If I believe You loved me enough to go to the cross, I have to believe You love me enough to catch me when my life or my ego seems out of control. Lord Jesus, I trust You. When my world and my mind are loud, when my eyes will not close, when my spirit is restless, Lord, by Your mercy, refresh me.*

Sorting It Out

Do you have trouble sleeping? Do you have trouble resting? If so, what's keeping you up? Is it physical? Is it spiritual? Mental? Emotional? And if this is an area in which you're not struggling, what kind of habits have you developed to make successful rest a priority? Please share these with your friends!

_____

_____

_____

List some things you do to relax and unwind. What makes you feel rested and refueled?

_____

_____

_____

Some seasons of life are busier or more difficult than others. Sometimes we're called to persevere through seasons like that. But if you find yourself burned out or trapped in a season where you've gone too long without a period of recovery, it may be time to look at your to-do list and repackage it. Pray about the possibility of calling in reinforcements, of cutting something out, or of shifting time away from something.

Spend a little time in prayer asking the Lord to help you depend on Him and the resources He sends for rest. Praise Him for His kindness and provision and care. Write your personal prayer in the space below.

_____

_____

_____

_____

_____

_____

_____

_____

_____

_____

_____

chapter 16

Instructions for Stuff We No Longer Own: Holding On and Letting Go

Monica Schmelter

> *When Jesus saw him lying there and knew that he had already been there a long time, he said to him,* "Do you want to be healed?" *The sick man answered him,* "Sir, I have no one to put me into the pool when the water is stirred up, and while I am going another steps down before me." *Jesus said to him,* "Get up, take up your bed, and walk." *And at once the man was healed, and he took up his bed and walked.*
> (John 5:6-9 ESV)

While I was working on selecting a topic for a series of television shows, I had the idea for *Lessons from the Junk Drawer*, the book you now have in your hand. As a part of my pre-production planning, I asked a group of brave women for pictures of their junk drawers. As I scanned through the pictures, I learned I wasn't the only one who had problems holding onto stuff.

I couldn't be certain, but I had serious doubts about whether Ann was making pop-tarts for her five children in a harvest gold two-slice toaster. I was also fairly sure Bobbi wasn't storing her almond milk in a 1972 side-by-side refrigerator. What is the deal with holding on to instruction manuals for stuff we no longer own anyway?

That's a question I can't answer. I do take great comfort in knowing that I am not alone. My junk drawer overflows with all kinds of instruction manuals. This is especially odd because I don't remember ever reading an instruction manual. Even when I end up with a few pieces left over while assembling an appliance, I am sure it's no big deal. Of course, I hang on to the few extra pieces just in case.

I Can't Help but Wonder

While basking in the knowledge that I am not alone in my instruction manual collection, I can't help but wonder what this phenomenon is all about. We all know that holding on to an instruction manual for a discarded appliance serves no useful purpose. It also takes up space and adds clutter to the junk drawer.

It's that way in our lives too. We hold on when it is no longer productive. It may be a past hurt, broken relationship, or another loss. We know it's over and even painful to hold on to, but we just can't muster up the strength let it go and move forward.

I can't help but wonder if that's a part of what the man at the pool of Bethesda experienced. He lived with a debilitating illness for years on end. I can only imagine his pain and frustration. The sound of the angel stirring the water must have been music to his ears. He just couldn't get there fast enough. By the time he got near the water someone else was already ahead of him. He was so close to his healing and yet so far. Was he too comfortable in the familiar?

Someone Always Beats Me to It

What we know for sure about the man at the pool of Bethesda was that he had a long-standing sickness—and a bed. When Jesus asked him to pick up his bed and walk he had to be stunned. Could he have thought, *What? Pick up the only thing that gives me comfort? By the way, Jesus, do you know what happens when I try to get up? I can't even get close to the water. Someone always beats me to it.*

The man at the pool of Bethesda wasn't holding onto an old instruction manual, but he did appear to have a problem letting go. He was so used to his illness, crippling though it was, that he hesitated to let go of life as he knew it and respond immediately to the healing words of Jesus.

I think I may understand why he responded like that to Jesus. He had been ill and unable to walk for a very long time. We all have experiences that shape how we think, feel, and behave. Letting go of the experiences that have shaped our lives, even to receive healing from Jesus, can seem unthinkable, even unrealistic.

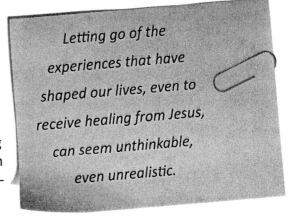

Letting go of the experiences that have shaped our lives, even to receive healing from Jesus, can seem unthinkable, even unrealistic.

While We Are Busy Holding On

I'm not sure how interested God is in our junk drawers (that's such good news), but I am confident He's very interested in seeing us pick up our beds and walk in freedom. While we are busy holding on, He invites us to let go and truly live.

"Therefore, since we are surrounded by so great a cloud of witnesses, let us also lay aside every weight, and sin which clings so closely, and let us run with endurance the race that is set before us, looking to Jesus, the founder and perfecter of our faith, who for the joy that was set before him endured the cross, despising the shame, and is seated at the right hand of the throne of God" (Hebrews 12:1-2).

One of the many lessons we learn from these two short verses of Scripture is that we are given the responsibility to lay aside every weight and sin. We are given the choice to run with endurance the race He sets before us. That's a big job isn't it? It's especially hard when we are holding on to baggage He's asked us to put down.

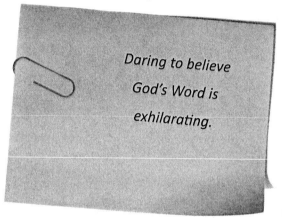

Daring to believe God's Word is exhilarating.

In a workout class I attended, the instructor asked us to wear a weighted vest. I learned quickly that additional weight made the workout much harder. In the health and fitness world, adding weight builds strength over time because we only wear that weight for a short time.

In the Christian race, running our course with excess baggage makes the trip harder and keeps us from the goodness God created.

Remember the man at the pool of Bethesda? He did not seem to understand how he could pick up his bed and leave his past behind. His circumstances and life experiences seemed more real to him than the words of Jesus. You may be in a similar position right now.

Perhaps grief over your foolish choice or prodigal child is a burden you carry every day. You cry in private and smile in public, but the pain is ever-present. Letting go of what you can't change doesn't erase the heartache, but it does lighten the load for living with joy today. Laying aside a weight or sin will equip you to run in God's honor.

His Word promises strength in our weakness and grace that is always sufficient. There comes a point when we have to pick up our bed and dare to believe God's Word.

"But he said to me, 'My grace is sufficient for you, for my power is made perfect in weakness.' Therefore I will boast all the more gladly of my weaknesses, so that the power of Christ may rest upon me" (2 Corinthians 12:9).

Daring to believe God's Word is exhilarating. It is also really hard work. It means acting on His Word rather than the circumstances we face every day. Sometimes everything within us is screaming, "Hold on for dear life!" while His still, small voice whispers "Let Go Now."

Clothes that Fit Ten Pounds Ago

All kinds of scenarios encourage us to hold on past the point of logic. How about the clothes in our closet that fit ten pounds ago? Or the tools in our garage we haven't needed for years? These items may draw crowds at yard sales, but they also set the stage for clutter in our homes and hearts.

I don't know if collecting instruction manuals does any more harm than taking up valuable space. I do know that in other cases, holding on too long can be detrimental to a healthy and productive life. Like most of life there is no one-size-fits-all answer for holding on and letting go protocols.

When it comes to cleaning out junk drawers, closets, etc., asking questions like "Have I used or needed this item in the last six months?" can be helpful in making the keep-or-toss decision. Weightier matters require more thought and consideration.

What Would It Look Like?

Holding on to God's promises and letting go of worldly attachments is the foundation for no-regret decisions. When I am in a challenging season, I often ask myself questions like: "How can I hold on to God's Word and let go of undue worry and concern?" "What does He want me to do about concerns that need action?" "What would it look like for me to dare to believe and relinquish all fear?"

For the man at the pool of Bethesda, this required him to pick up the bed that brought him comfort and walk. He had to dare to believe the words of Jesus were so powerful that he could literally walk away from his past.

God's Word is still that powerful. He calls us to hold on to truth of His Word and let go of all the world's lies. Whether you need to let go of the shame of your past, a habit of today, or your fear of tomorrow, His grace is always sufficient. His all-sufficient grace is a beautifully recurring theme in this book. Letting go of what you don't need and holding onto that grace may not always be easy, but it will be worth it.

Sorting it Out

Do I need to let go of anything? If so what? How?

_____

_____

_____

How can I hold on to the truth of God's Word and let go of the world's lies?

_____

_____

_____

What would it look like for me to dare to believe God's Word in every area of my life?

_____

_____

_____

List some of the promises you can hold on to as you dare to believe His Word.

_____
_____
_____

chapter 17

Sticky Notes: The Math of Sticking to Jesus

Rhonda Rhea

*God's readiness to give and forgive is now
public. Salvation's available for everyone!
We're being shown how to turn our backs
on a godless, indulgent life, and how to take
on a God-filled, God-honoring life. This new
life is starting right now, and is whetting our
appetites for the glorious day when our great
God and Savior, Jesus Christ, appears.*
(Titus 2:11-13 The Message)

Anyone else find a rainbow of sticky notes in the junk drawer? I have post-its in every color, size and shape. I don't think I could count all these note pads even if I weren't terrible at math.

When we were raising our five children, the sticky note stash was not nearly so plentiful. Those things were like gold, and somehow my kids knew that. I'm a list person. I needed those notes, people. I had to hide them away like so much list-booty.

I do remember a toddler of mine finding my stash. By the time I got to him, I could hardly find that baby. Have you ever seen a walking sticky note? It was hilarious. Not many parts of the room were left note-less either. So many notes.

That's My Story and I'm Sticking to It

Oh the noteworthy math of motherhood. Of course, anytime you're talking math and you put me into the equation, you're going to have some incongruencies. They've been there since I was a kid myself.

When I was in junior high, anytime I felt like I needed a good cry, I'd just ask my dad to help me with my math.

> Our sin nature often loves to adjust the equation, trying to force God's plan to fit our own handy-at-the-moment wishes.

I'd like to say something about the sums—or is it sins— of the fathers right here, but any way you pun it, it was actually all me. Even in high school, I remember going up to my algebra teacher's desk saying, "Mr. Showalter, I'm stuck on number 5." At which point he would do the problem for me with a smile. Mind you, I was also stuck on numbers one through four, but I didn't want to overwhelm the man.

From early on, I understood that there was a reason they were called math problems. The stages of grief over math ineptitude went something like this: 1) Denial. 2) Trying to bargain—but let's face it, bargaining can require math, so... 4) Realizing there was probably a missing step. What number are we on again? and 7) I really want a sandwich.

There was always something I would rather do than math problems. And those somethings were big-time distractions.

I wish I'd thought to call them weapons of math disruption but I was probably too distracted. Sometimes I had a choice between picking up that math book and finding myself stuck on number 5, or instead...sandwich.

Between Some Math and a Stuck Place

Ever feel a little stuck? Sometimes it's about studying a problem long enough to decipher what to do next. It seems like it's even more often that we're stuck because we know what we're supposed to do next, but we've lost count and let someone, or something, whisk away our attention and energies. Stuck.

God's chosen people have a recorded history of more than a few instances of stuck-ness. Many of their rock-and-a-hard-place kinds of experiences were a result of not being obedient to what the Lord had commanded them to do. One little distraction, then one little compromise that turned into another, that turned into another, and—well, you get the math. One compromise after another turns into...stuck.

Compromise is trading God's will for us for something that our flesh wants instead. We assume it will still add up to give the answer we seek. But it can't. Our sin nature often loves to adjust the equation, trying to force God's plan to fit our own handy-at-the-moment wishes. Talk about not adding up. It's just plain sin.

Our call is to obey Him. When we choose to follow distractions or compromise, we're denying His grace. Paul said, "For the grace of God has appeared with salvation for all people,

Maybe this is all a good reminder that the infinite God who created numbers and who fits them together in all kinds of creative ways uses math to show us Himself.

instructing us to deny godlessness and worldly lusts and to live in a sensible, righteous, and godly way in the present age, while we wait for the blessed hope and appearing of the glory of our great God and Savior, Jesus Christ. He gave Himself for us to redeem us from all lawlessness and to cleanse for Himself a people for His own possession, eager to do good works," (Titus 2:11-14 HCSB).

The God Beyond Numbers

To deny His grace is to compromise. To compromise is to deny His grace. The same grace that saved us. It's also that very grace that is training us to say no to compromise. No to sin. Yes to cleansing. Yes to good works.

Training in refusing to compromise is an integral part of living well. Even though "integral" sounds a little "math-ey." Maybe this is all a good reminder that the infinite God who created numbers and who fits them together in all kinds of creative ways uses math to show us Himself. Even me. How does my infinite God astound me? Let me count the ways.

Counting, listing, numbering—math-ing—I had to pull them all out big-time in those years of kid-raising. I'm not a structured person by nature. But to-do lists became my friends. And enemies.

Teach a Mom to List

On any given day, I made a gargantuan list, then had to quick-plan for a dozen things that weren't on it. Things that weren't on any list. Ever.

Five children. On any given day, I made a gargantuan list, then had to quick-plan for a dozen things that weren't on it. Things that weren't on any list. Ever. Who can plan, for instance, for an away-from-home potty-training disaster you're forced to clean up with three Wal-Mart receipts, last week's church bulletin, and a Kit Kat wrapper (give me a break).

As they got older, I had to make time for other things I didn't expect. Like listening to them learn the trumpet or watching them do that card trick. Again.

Teach a man to fish and it's all good. But teach a kid a card trick and be prepared to watch it nonstop for like 12 years.

"Is this your card?"—'til college.

Our time raising children is short. I can get philosophical about it, for sure. I've long said, when one door opens, another door opens. And then also a side door. All the doors. And they never close. Because you have kids.

I wonder how many months of my life I spent closing doors behind this or that kid running in or out. I had those five babies in seven years. That means in a 12-year span I probably slept four hours. Total. Essentially, I traded sleep for door-closing. It's a thought that makes me smile. And it makes me want a nap.

Come and Nap

Ever feel like your soul needs a nap? Jesus knew you would. He said, "Come to me, all of you who are weary and burdened, and I will give you rest. Take my yoke and learn from me, because I am lowly and humble in heart, and you will find rest for your souls. For my yoke is easy and my burden is light," (Matthew 11:28-30 CSB).

Rest for our bodies. We do have to make time for that. But soul rest is at least as vital. The math there is not as tricky as we sometimes try to make it. Anytime we find ourselves feeling burned out, weary, burdened—heavy—it's time to step back and listen to Jesus' call to "Come to me." It's an open door. And to our delight, it stays open.

When you're frantically adding up and sorting one to-do list from another (is this your card?) and when your mind feels cluttered and weighted down with challenges and stresses, remember your Savior's reminder that He waits for you. He will be your respite, your comfort, your encouragement—your strength to obey and to take your next step. All you need to do is come.

The Best Is Yet To Come

Come to Him in prayer. Come to Him in worship. Come to Him through His Word. Give Him the first-fruits of your time. Lay down a burdensome yoke you've placed on yourself or someone has put on you. And you'll find the perspective you're looking for. So often all the urgent to-dos sort themselves out as we remember His call to come, to exchange our plan for the just-fits comfort of His will. Would you believe, even when an unexpected disaster thrusts itself upon your list, you can still smile. His easy yoke comes with grace, joy, peace—everything you need for a genuine, successful existence.

Responding to His "come to Me" should top my every list. Relief from my own exhausting yoke. Strength and renewal under His yoke.

The Real Answer to the Biggest Problem

The answer to the problem of getting stuck in compromise or unfruitfulness is always rest. That very specific kind of rest. Resting in God alone. Then you can obey with energy. Any other kind of spiritual math will never add up.

For the right kind of following and right kind of resting? Oh yes. I'm sticking to Jesus.

Sorting It Out

Is there a problem that's leaving you with that stuck feeling? Is it that you don't know what to do next, or is it one of those stuck instances when you've let something distract you from what you already know to do? What needs to happen to get back on track?

_____

_____

_____

What are some of the compromises that tend to hold people back? What is the best way to say "No" to those?

_____

_____

_____

How does a day look different when resting in Jesus tops our to-do list?

_____

_____

_____

How will you respond to His "come to Me" this very day?

_____

_____

_____

Kids' Meal Toy: It Comes with the Meal

Kaley Rhea

> *This resurrection life you received from God is not a timid, grave-tending life. It's adventurously expectant, greeting God with a childlike "What's next, Papa?" God's Spirit touches our spirits and confirms who we really are. We know who he is, and we know who we are: Father and children.*
> (Romans 8:15-16 The Message)

Who doesn't find a couple kids' meal toys in the ol' junk drawer? I don't even have kids, and I've got some in there. Usually missing an arm or a wheel or something. Fiddled with or fought over for six to eleven minutes before it gets broken or loses its appeal and gets tossed in a drawer or a toy box or under a bed like pre-trash.

Poor Kids' Meal Toys

Brightly-colored plastic with poorly-placed stickers. Badly-rendered details. Made to give away. Not meant to satisfy.

The best you can hope for as one of these is an existence spent inside a sealed plastic bag where nothing can get to you. The most value you could possibly bring in is an Ebay best offer + free shipping. And that probably only if you're trademarked™.

Someone might choose a meal based on the prospect of getting a toy. But no one chooses the toy. It's never something a kid would pick out at a store or spend time treasuring. It's a default. An add-on. Extra.

You ever identify with this? You know, metaphorically? Feel unseen. Untalented. Unchosen. Unloved. Not even trademarked probably.

I get it. I know all those feelings. But this metaphor is wrong. I can think of a better one.

You're not the toy in this scenario. You're the child.

Baby Dolls

You ever identify with this? You know, metaphorically? Feel unseen. Untalented. Unchosen. Unloved. Not even trademarked probably. I get it.

Romans 8:14-17 reads, "For all who are led by the Spirit of God are sons of God. For you did not receive the spirit of slavery to fall back into fear, but you have received the Spirit of adoption as sons, by whom we cry, "Abba! Father!"

The Spirit himself bears witness with our spirit that we are children of God, and if children, then heirs—heirs of God and fellow heirs with Christ, provided we suffer with him in order that we may also be glorified with him."

You are the child walking into the McRestaurant, holding onto her daddy's hand, one thousand percent secure in the knowledge that she is safe and will be fed and cherished. Not because she's spent her child life earning it. But because *he* has proven all her child life—through every hard time, through all her moments of disobedience and rebellion—that he is a good dad. "What's next, Papa?"

Isn't it interesting how God designed family relationships to illustrate to us who He is? To demonstrate parts of His character? I'm in love with that. I mean, I know far too often, we mess this up and hurt each other, and our relationships don't mirror His because we're imperfect. But the roots—the things that make strong families strong. The things we long for. The things we know are good about family and togetherness and dependence and sacrifice and lovingkindness—all of them are lessons about the character of the enormously complex God who has with gracious simplicity called Himself our Father.

The Creator God who moved the psalmist to write in Psalm 139:13-16, "For you formed my inward parts; you knitted me together in my mother's womb. I praise you, for I am fearfully and wonderfully made. Wonderful are your works; my soul knows it very well. My frame was not hidden from you, when I was being made in secret, intricately woven in the depths of the earth. Your eyes saw my unformed substance; in your book were written, every one of them, the days that were formed for me, when as yet there was none of them."

You were knitted! I don't know much about knitting, but I know it takes yarn and love. You were fashioned and planned out and on purpose. God saw You always, and He sees You now.

Action Figures

When you doubt God meant it when He made you, when You doubt you are loved when you have

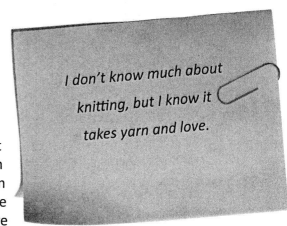

I don't know much about knitting, but I know it takes yarn and love.

messed up, when you doubt the Lord has placed on your life a calling and a purpose that is eternally significant, when you feel like an extra or an add-on rather than the beloved child of God who was made by Him and then adopted through the greatest sacrifice in all of history, step back. Read these words. Think about these words. Shout these words. I'm not even kidding:

> "Blessed be the God and Father of our Lord Jesus Christ, who has blessed us in Christ with every spiritual blessing in the heavenly places, even as he chose us in him before the foundation of the world, that we should be holy and blameless before him. In love he predestined us for adoption to himself as sons through Jesus Christ, according to the purpose of his will, to the praise of his glorious grace, with which he has blessed us in the Beloved. In him we have redemption through his blood, the forgiveness of our trespasses, according to the riches of his grace, which he lavished upon us, in all wisdom and insight making known to us the mystery of his will, according to his purpose, which he set forth in Christ as a plan for the fullness of time, to unite all things in him, things in heaven and things on earth. In him we have obtained an inheritance, having been predestined according to the purpose of him who works all things according to the counsel of his will." (Ephesians 1:3-11)

If you do shout that passage from Paul's letter to the church at Ephesus, make sure to take a breath at every comma. Paul don't stop, and he don't play. God chose you. God loves your personhood. God has a plan for you.

Read it again. I know it's long, and I'm not trying to tell you what to do, but this is better and more real than anything

I could begin to know how say to you, wherever you are. It's truth. It's Gospel. It's wisdom. It's forever. It's happiness. It's stirring. It's healing. It's life.

Tea Party Sets

Let me pause here to tell you that if you haven't accepted this gift yet—if you've never placed your faith in Christ, placed your hand in His, given Him control and said, "Father, You lead"—I want to invite you. The invitation comes from Him and has your name on it. I just want to pass it along.

> "But now the righteousness of God has been manifested apart from the law, although the Law and the Prophets bear witness to it—the righteousness of God through faith in Jesus Christ for all who believe. For there is no distinction: for all have sinned and fall short of the glory of God, and are justified by his grace as a gift, through the redemption that is in Christ Jesus" (Romans 3:21-24).

You believe Jesus is the perfect Son of God, that He came to the earth as a man two thousand odd years ago, and that according to His perfect plan, He died in our place, taking our sin with Him, and three days later came back to life, defeating death. Say something like this to Him from your heart:

> *Heavenly Father, I'm amazed by the mercy and love You've shown me. I believe You created me. I believe You when You say You want me. I'm sorry for all the ways I've fallen short. I'm sorry for the things I've done that have hurt You and hurt people. Thank You for loving me anyway. For choosing to die for me anyway. I accept Your gift. I believe You are Truth. For the rest of my life, by Your Holy Spirit, all I want to*

do is praise You, serve You, honor You, glorify You, and follow You. Whatever comes my way in this life, I trust You are bigger, and I trust that with each step I'll get to know You better. And I am giddy-excited for the day I see You face to face. Thank You, precious Jesus, and in Your holy name, Amen.

Whether you are a brand-new Christian or one who has known Jesus for many seasons, I'm so happy you're here. I need you. I need you loving Jesus where you are as much as I need me loving Jesus where I am. An interesting side-effect of being adopted of God and joint heirs with Christ is you get this really cool and diverse family of believers, too.

Fair warning, the family of God can be loud and sometimes obnoxious, and all of them are wrong about as often as you are, which is more often than any of us would like to think. But congratulations, they're yours. I encourage you to connect. To learn and teach and love on each other a lot.

Also I am your actual nerd sister, and I *will* play Ninja Turtles with you.

Fair warning, the family of God can be loud and sometimes obnoxious, and all of them are wrong about as often as you are, more often than any of us would like to think.

Sorting It Out

List some attributes of God's character you see Him demonstrate in Scripture. You may need extra paper. That's cool.

_____
_____
_____
_____
_____
_____

Now, having been reminded of the vastness and greatness of the God who has made and loved you, list some things that are true about you and your own identity.

_____
_____
_____

How reassuring to know we are not the enemies of God or the playthings of God. We are the children of God. Write a little prayer of thanks, as general or specific as you like, to the God who wasn't content with the titles of King or Master. Thank Him for wanting to be called Father.

_____
_____
_____
_____
_____
_____

chapter 19

Matches: Light Your World with His Love

Monica Schmelter

*So the woman left her water jar and went
away into town and said to the people,
"Come, see a man who told me all that I ever
did. Can this be the Christ?"
They went out of the town and
were coming to him.*
(John 4:28-30)

When I was a little girl, I remember the warning not to play with matches. Thankfully, I never did. I do remember the joy of birthday parties and the scramble to find a book of matches to light the candles. Why did my parents look in the junk drawer last?

Little did I know as a child about the good kind of fire that could be lit in your heart when you make Jesus your Savior. When I was fourteen years old, I started the 9th grade in a private Christian school. I wasn't a Christian and I had zero interest in believing the Bible. My parents thought a Christian school would be a good idea for a troubled teen like me. They hoped it would help me meet a different crowd of people and make better decisions.

On a Mission to Ruin my Life

By the time I was thirteen I had already run away from home. I skipped school frequently and experimented with drugs occasionally. Clearly I wasn't on a good path, but you couldn't convince me of that. I thought my teachers, counselors, and parents were on a mission to cramp my style and ruin my life.

The days seemed long at my small Christian school. I deemed chapel as boring and the dress code a fashion disaster. The students were friendly enough, but I thought I had nothing in common with them.

Unfazed by My Tough Exterior

There was one particular student named Leslie who went out of her way to connect with me. She seemed unfazed by my tough exterior. One day she handed me a really cute card. Inside the card she wrote "I am praying for you." I appreciated the card, but I turned around and complained to fellow classmates that I didn't want to be bothered by that Jesus stuff.

I'm not sure why, but when Leslie invited me to a movie night at her church, I said yes. I guess I sensed in her the genuine care I yearned for. This meant I would ride the bus home with her after school and then go to church with her that evening. I remember the movie touched my heart. When the movie was over the pastor asked us to bow our heads. With heads bowed, he asked us to raise our hands if we wanted prayer. I lifted my hand. When the pastor asked all who raised their hands to come forward, I did not budge.

Several weeks later my family was invited to church by a friend of my mom's. This time my whole family, including my Muslim grandfather, his second wife and their four children, attended as well. The church was hosting a healing service. My younger brother has Downs' Syndrome and was hospitalized frequently for other health-related ailments. Out of love for my brother, we all attended the service. I hadn't been to church often and this particular service seemed unusual. People were clapping, singing loudly, and raising their hands in the air. I had never seen this before and feared they might be crazy.

The Same Nudge

Later in the service they prayed for my brother. Shortly after the prayer for healing, they extended a call for all who wanted to accept Christ as Savior. Much to my surprise and chagrin, I felt a nudge. The same nudge I experienced at Leslie's church. I fought it for a bit and then stood up and walked quickly down the aisle. With tears streaming down my face, I knelt at the altar and gave my heart to Christ.

After the service, my brother was never hospitalized again. My family did not continue attending church. However, my parents graciously drove me to services every Sunday and Wednesday. I went from troubled teen to on fire with the love of Christ. There was no earthly explanation for the change. It was simply a miracle that everyone I knew noticed.

My seat in church was on the third row right next to Mrs. Gardner, the pastors' wife. I was an avid note-taker and paid very close attention. I knew my life depended on it. One Sunday my pastor preached a sermon using Psalm 2:8: "Ask of me, and I shall give thee the heathen for

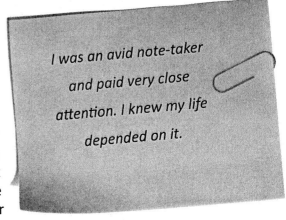

I was an avid note-taker and paid very close attention. I knew my life depended on it.

thine inheritance, and the uttermost parts of the earth for thy possession" (KJV).

When Pastor Gardner explained that I could rewrite the history of my family through prayer, my heart was lit on fire with passion and excitement. I started believing that my family and friends would all eventually come to faith in Christ. After that sermon, I wrote the Psalm 2:8 scripture on the top of several pieces of loose leaf paper. Then I started writing the names of my family and friends down under the scripture verse. I prayed over the names daily. Then my list got so long I put it in a box for safekeeping. Over the years, I started calling the box my prayer box.

My Muslim Grandfather Accepted Christ

It's been more than 40 years since I heard that sermon and started my prayer box. I've seen most of my family, including my Muslim grandfather, come to Christ. I continue to pray for the others. When I reflect on God's goodness to a rebellious and stubborn teenager, I am overwhelmed with gratitude. Our Father's love expressed through His only Son, Jesus Christ, is more than amazing.

In this politically correct and easily offended culture it can seem overwhelming to share the love of Christ. Go ahead and do it anyway. It only takes a few sparks to ignite a flame, so get out your matches and light away. Sure, the winds of adversity and persecution may come your way. Don't be afraid of that. If one match gets blown out, light another one. The Bible says it's a great honor to be persecuted. "Blessed are you when others revile you and persecute you and utter all kinds of evil against you falsely on my account. Rejoice and be glad, for your reward is great in heaven, for so they persecuted the prophets who were before you" (Matthew 5:11-12).

Have you considered the great reward that awaits us when we endure persecution? I think back to Leslie who first reached out to me. At the time, I did not show appreciation for her concern or prayers. I responded with indifference—a kind of persecution for Leslie. But for Leslie, sharing Christ with me was more important to her than my response. That is the key to sharing the light of Christ with your world. Christ has to be more important to you than the person's response.

I Found Her on Facebook

A few years ago, I taped a television show about evangelism and persecution. When we filmed that show I couldn't stop thinking about Leslie. She was the first one to witness to me. Where would I be without Leslie's boldness? More than 40 years had passed, but I wanted to find her and say thank you. I was ecstatic when I found her on Facebook. I messaged her and expressed my appreciation and apologized for my poor behavior. She was very gracious in her response. She and I keep in touch now. We pray for one another, and we also encourage each other to stay bold and share Christ every opportunity we get.

I often think about the woman at the well. We don't even know her name. We do know she had five husbands followed by a live-in. We also know after she met Christ a fire was lit in her heart that couldn't be extinguished. She went back into the city telling everyone she met about the Messiah.

Have you ever thought about what that might have cost her? She went back into the city where people probably knew all about her. They knew her past. No doubt many of them felt she should live in shame. Her lifestyle wouldn't make headlines in our culture, or in some aspects of biblical culture, but it certainly did in her hometown. Even so, the power of meeting Christ was stronger than her past and present. When our hearts are lit on fire with the love of Christ we are unstoppable.

Rewrite Your Family History

We can all rewrite the history of our families with the power of love and prayer. We can light our world with the power of

Christ by daring to share His love without undue concern over the response. Even Jesus got persecuted. The Bible teaches us that no student is greater than his teacher. The Bible also teaches us that all our efforts in faith will be richly rewarded.

It's never wise to play with physical matches. But it's very wise to allow the love of Christ to ignite a flame in your heart that burns so brightly it extinguishes the darkness.

Sorting It Out

How are you allowing the love of Christ to ignite a fire in your life? If not, how could you change that?

_____
_____
_____
_____
_____

Do you have any family members or friends that don't know Christ yet? If yes, are you praying for them regularly? If yes, are you looking for opportunities to show the love of Christ and to share Christ with them?

_____
_____
_____
_____
_____
_____

Do you fear or have you experienced persecution? What has that been like for you?

_____
_____
_____
_____
_____
_____

Would having a prayer box or something similar help you re-member to pray for your family/friends that aren't saved yet? What else might you use?

_____

_____

_____

_____

_____

_____

chapter 20

Pens: Pens, Pens and More Pens—Leaving a Genuine Mark

Rhonda Rhea

*Do not be conformed to this world, but be
transformed by the renewal of your mind, that
by testing you may discern what is the will of
God, what is good and acceptable and perfect.*
(Romans 12:2)

Black pen, blue pen, old pen, new pen, leaky pen, dry pen, freaky pen, eye pen.

Wait, that last one wasn't a pen. Make a note. But do it with one of those other pens, not with the eye pencil.

What's an eye-lining pencil doing mixed in with all my pens anyway? My schedule is crazy and makeup sometimes happens on the go. Evidently the makeup doesn't always make it back into the makeup bag. I do, however, make it a point not to confuse my eyeliner pencil with permanent markers. There are lines we simply should not cross.

Some High-Brow Humor?

I do take my eye-lining rather seriously. Someone once told me that all crazy women have super-thin eyebrows. I don't see how I could even begin to argue with that logic. So I pencil. And I pencil strong. I feel I have a lot to prove. Or disprove. Or at least not confirm.

That's one reason doing makeup in the car is such risky business. One hard stop and a gal could end up with a seriously high eyebrow. No one could ever be as astonished as that kind of brow implies. And yes, please excuse me if the humor here is a bit...ah...*highbrow*.

Not long ago, even full-well knowing the risk, I was doing my makeup in the car. Kaley and I were traveling. She was driving and hit a bad bump at a very crucial eyebrow moment. I immediately shot her a half-angry look. Not because I was really angry. Hey, bumps happen. I gave her the look because suddenly I had one fiercely anger-shaped brow. That's hard to get rid of. To find some sort of symmetry I had to line and over-line *both* eyebrows. We're talking, eyebrows full on. Like, high-beam on. I just combed my bangs extra low and hoped people would read between the lines, as it were. Goofy road-bump.

Comparatively Speaking

If anyone knew about bumps in the road, it was Paul. Talk about some hardships. It was enough to furrow any brow. But in Romans 8:18 he tells us that he chooses to see those difficulties as no big deal. "For I consider that the sufferings of this present time are not worth comparing with the glory that is to be revealed to us."

Difficulties, persecution, heartaches? Temporary. But the glory? It's forever! We've talked about the difficulties, but let's zero in on our future for a minute. Our future is so much brighter than anything dark we could ever encounter here. What hope! A few verses further down in Romans we read, "we ourselves, who have the firstfruits of the Spirit, groan inwardly as we wait eagerly for adoption as sons, the redemption of our bodies. For in this hope we were saved. Now hope that is seen is not hope. For who hopes for what he sees? But if we hope for what we do not see, we wait for it with patience" (vv. 23-25). It's the very hope in which we were saved!

Hope reminds us that we live between the times. We can't see the big picture full-beam. We're living in that space between the bumps in the road and the glory that awaits. But this we know. We can walk in faith and live in confidence even now because our Father has a great plan for our future. He is a trustworthy God who keeps His promises. That means we can wait with assurance—eager, yet patient.

We were not promised a life of ease, every little line drawn oh so perfectly, on this side of eternity. Quite the opposite, in fact. We were, however, promised courage straight from the Father, we were promised everything we need to enjoy this life here and to endure the not so enjoyable aspects of this world. We were promised a holy calling and a greater purpose—a life that matters here, now and forever. Ask any mommy. The scribbliest scribbles can make the most beautiful art.

"For God did not give us a spirit of timidity *or* cowardice *or* fear, but [He has given us a spirit] of power and of love and of sound judgment *and* personal discipline [abilities that result in a calm, well-balanced mind and self-control]. So do not be ashamed to testify about our Lord or about me His prisoner, but with me take your share of suffering for the gospel [continue to preach regardless of the circumstances], in accordance with the power of God [for His power is invincible], for He delivered us *and* saved us and called us with a holy calling [a calling that leads to a consecrated life—a life set apart—a life of purpose], not because of our works [or because of any personal merit—we could do nothing to earn this], but because of His own purpose and grace [His amazing, undeserved favor] which was granted to us in Christ Jesus before the world began [eternal ages ago]" (2 Timothy 1:7-9 AMP).

Reading Between the Lines—And Living Between the Times

We have a better perspective on life and its challenges when we think about our future and about the things that matter in the here and now—a well-balanced mind, a consecrated life, works that are a thank-you to God and not an earning. We're able to focus less on the things that won't matter in eternity and more on the things of God. Jonathan Edwards, great revival preacher of the 1700's, prayed, "O Lord, stamp eternity on my eyeballs."

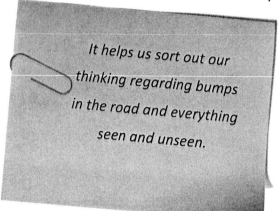

It helps us sort out our thinking regarding bumps in the road and everything seen and unseen.

Stamping eternity on our eyeballs is not about pencils or brows. It's about keeping our eyes God-ward and staying ever-mindful of our future with Him, with His holy agenda at the heart of all we do. It keeps us mindful of those around us who need Jesus.

It helps us sort out our thinking regarding bumps in the road and everything seen and unseen. It helps us become a testimony to others. It builds a legacy. We're in this world, yes, but it's good to know where to draw the line.

Knowing where to draw the line? Here's a little reminder that that's also good for eyebrows.

Sorting It Out

Thinking about your own legacy, what would you like to be remembered for most?

_____

_____

_____

Take a look at Paul's account of his "thorn in the flesh" in the Amplified Version of 2 Corinthians 12:7-10.

> "Because of the surpassing greatness _and_ extraordinary nature of the revelations [which I received from God], for this reason, to keep me from thinking of myself as important, a thorn in the flesh was given to me, a messenger of Satan, to torment _and_ harass me—to keep me from exalting myself! Concerning this I pleaded with the Lord three times that it might leave me; but He has said to me, 'My grace is sufficient for you [My lovingkindness and My mercy are more than enough—always available—regardless of the situation]; for [My] power is being perfected [and is completed and shows itself most effectively] in [your] weakness.' Therefore, I will all the more gladly boast in my weaknesses, so that the power of Christ [may completely enfold me and] may dwell in me. So I am well pleased with weaknesses, with insults, with distresses, with persecutions, and with difficulties, for the sake of Christ; for when I am weak [in human strength], then I am strong [truly able, truly powerful, truly drawing from God's strength]"

What were Paul's reasons for remaining content? How do you think that affected, influenced, and left a mark on those around him?

_____

_____

_____

How has the testimony of faith you've seen in others who are good at living between the times influenced you? Have those people left a mark on you? Can you think of ways your ability to focus on Christ, eyes on Him, may have left a mark on others?

_____

_____

_____

Here's another passage that compels us to fix our eyes on our victory in Christ. These are the peace-giving words of Jesus Himself. Read this one in the Amplified as well, then list what you have and what you can do because of your all-powerful, victorious Savior.

> "I have told you these things, so that in Me you may have [perfect] peace. In the world you have tribulation *and* distress *and* suffering, but be courageous [be confident, be undaunted, be filled with joy]; I have overcome the world. [My conquest is accomplished, My victory abiding]" (John 16:33 AMP).

_____

_____

_____

"I know how great this makes you feel, even though you have to put up with every kind of aggravation in the meantime. Pure gold put in the fire comes out of it proved pure; genuine faith put through this suffering comes out proved genuine. When Jesus wraps this all up, it's your faith, not your gold, that God will have on display as evidence of his victory" (1 Peter 1:6-7 The Message)

Old Lipsticks: Smack in the Middle of His Grace

Kaley Rhea

*For we do not have a high priest who is unable
to sympathize with our weaknesses, but one
who in every respect has been tempted as
we are, yet without sin. Let us then with
confidence draw near to the throne of
grace, that we may receive mercy and
find grace to help in time of need.*
(Hebrews 4:15-16)

It doesn't feel like I buy a lot of lipsticks. So how is it I have so many? And when did I decide I definitely needed this electric shade of purple? Although, now that I see it, I know there's going to be a random Thursday morning in my near future where I'm heading out the door for work, and I think, *You know what? I am not ruled by earth tones. Today's a day for a bold lip.*

Looking at my rainbow of dollar store lip colors reminds me of the prismatic, multi-faceted grace of my God. And it calls to mind a certain biblical figure as well. You know. That

Old Testament story about a guy. There was a boat involved. Seems really appropriate to talk about him when we're talking about the *colorful* grace of God. You see where I'm going with this?

No, not Noah. I' m talking about my boy Jonah!

Lip One-Liners and Gloss

I could talk about the book of Jonah all day. It's amazing. If you have time, read through it right now. It's honestly got a smaller word count than this chapter. The book is a mere four Bible chapters of mayhem and peril and miracles and emotional sad-boy fit-throwing. If it comes down to a choice between reading that and reading this chapter, read Jonah. You can come back to this later.

Let's hit a few of the major plot points. Chapter one launches with God telling Jonah to go to Nineveh. Jonah without hesitation took every step necessary to flee by ship in the opposite direction. Storm came up, and after the sailors found out Jonah was the reason for that storm, Jonah's like "Ahem. Yes, that's for me." He convinced the sailors on the ship to throw him overboard into the sea. Where he would've died except for a great fish.

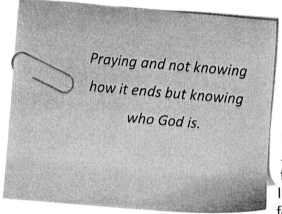

Praying and not knowing how it ends but knowing who God is.

Chapter two: Inside a fish. The storybooks usually depict it like a great cavernous space with a little island where he's got a shelter and a small fire while he's praying to be released because it smells bad. I don't know, but I kind of imagine a tighter fit and wonder if Jonah didn't feel like he was sitting blind and hard-pressed to breathe trapped in a fish-flesh coffin. Three days and nights. Praying and not knowing how it ends but knowing who God is. Then God has words with the fish, who has been making its way across the sea, and it throws Jonah up on dry land.

Then there's chapter three. Jonah came out of the water, all crinkled and torn up and fish-kissed with coral blue number two high gloss lipstick. Sick.

God told him again to go to Nineveh. This time he went.

You know what's next. "And the people of Nineveh believed God (Jonah 3:5a)." The news reached all the way up to the king, and he moved. He mobilized. He proclaimed to his whole great city an Old Testament version of "We need to repent now, and we need to repent hard."

Think about this. What preacher ever gets to see Jonah's level of success? How many ministers go to a place that is so morally bankrupt nobody thinks they're worth the trip, preaches there for a little bit, and the whole place says, "Actually...I think you're right," and then they change? This is a miracle! This is the kind of tale missionaries dream about and pray for and very seldom get the opportunity to witness. What an incredible privilege!

And did Jonah fall to his knees in awe of his powerful, gracious Lord? Is chapter four full of Jonah getting poetic describing how overwhelmed he was by the blessing of being used of God to bring about such a miraculous transformation that saves the lives of actual thousands? Nuh uh. Nope. Not our Jonah. No, he's going to lecture God on how compassionate He is. He's going to I-told-you-so God.

"O Lord, is not this what I said when I was yet in my country? That is why I made haste to flee to Tarshish; for I knew that you are a gracious God and merciful, slow to anger and abounding in steadfast love, and relenting from disaster. Therefore now, O Lord, please take my life from me, for it is better for me to die than to live" (Jonah 4:2).

Wow.

Talk About a Bold Lip

This from the same man who a few days previous while stuck inside a live fish, gave a whole glorious freestyle rap in Jonah 2:2-9 about his gracious God of mercy and steadfast love:

> "I called out to the Lord, out of my distress, and he answered me; out of the belly of Sheol I cried, and you heard my voice. For you cast me into the deep, into the heart of the seas, and the flood surrounded me; all your waves and your billows passed over me. Then I said, 'I am driven away from your sight; yet I shall again look upon your holy temple.' The waters closed in over me to take my life;the deep surrounded me; weeds were wrapped about my head at the roots of the mountains. I went down to the land whose bars closed upon me forever; yet you brought up my life from the pit, O Lord my God. When my life was fainting away, I remembered the Lord, and my prayer came to you, into your holy temple. Those who pay regard to vain idols forsake their hope of steadfast love. But I with the voice of thanksgiving will sacrifice to you; what I have vowed I will pay. Salvation belongs to the Lord!"

"Salvation Belongs to the Lord." But in chapter 4 Jonah seethed a diatribe wanting salvation to belong to him instead.

Mwah!

What's amazing about this book isn't Jonah. Because Jonah is all of us. I can think of few examples in the Bible of a person who represents me to my very core and is at the same time a completely ridiculous human.

What's amazing throughout these chapters is God. How gracious He is. How many chances He gives. How He rescues, how He relents, how He forgives. How He asks with shocking tenderness like a Dad, "Do you do well to be angry?" "Do you do well to be angry for [this]?"

Jonah cried, "Yes!"

Even while the rest of us reading are thinking, "No, man. You don't do well at all."

Way too often, I'm the one trying to reason with the Lord that my way is right, and His way should yield. Even while there's the whole of human history (and my own personal history) standing just out of earshot behind me, collectively shouting "*Really?*"

God's grace is sufficient when you're caught in a quagmire you've built of your own disobedience.

Jonah is all of us. And thankfully, God is none of us. Which sounds kind of like Ninevehs. Which is neither here nor there.

This is the God who, centuries after Jonah lived and died, moved Paul to write the passage we just examined in chapter 20 of *Messy to Meaningful*: 2 Corinthians 12:9, "But He [the Lord] said to me, 'My grace is sufficient for you, for My power is made perfect in weakness.'"

God's grace is sufficient when you're caught in a quagmire you've built of your own disobedience. God's grace is sufficient when you're caught in a circumstance built of someone else's cruelty or foolishness. God's grace is sufficient when you do well. God's grace is sufficient when you don't.

God's grace is infinitely more brilliant than any high gloss or satin finish lip stuff. And it lasts longer, too.

Sorting It Out

You know who is the opposite of Jonah in almost every way? Jesus. Jesus, Who had all the compassion and grace that Jonah didn't. Jesus, Who did not run. Jesus, Who spent three days inside a tomb we had earned. Jesus, "who, though He was in the form of God did not consider equality with God something to be grasped, but emptied himself, by taking the form of a servant, being born in the likeness of men. And being found in human form, He humbled Himself by becoming obedient to the point of death, even death on a cross" (Philippians 2:6-8).

Write a prayer of thanksgiving to God, and ask Him to make you more like Jesus.

_____

_____

_____

_____

_____

_____

When Jonah tried to hide from God, he ran toward Tarshish, on the opposite end of the known world from Nineveh. Is there any part of your heart that likes to vacation at a timeshare in Tarshish? Spend some time with God asking Him to reveal the things in your life you may be trying to hide or deny. Repent and trust His grace and His promises.

_____

_____

_____

_____

_____

_____

The book of Jonah ends terribly abruptly for me. Like I really want to know Jonah's response to God's words here. But it almost doesn't matter. Jonah's emotions are so all over the map (literally), that whatever he said in that moment he may have forgotten by the next day. I can be like that, too. When I feel close to God, my response is badly-composed but heart-felt love poems, and when I feel angry or hard done by, I sound like a grown adult baby.

Take a few moments here to remember God's faithfulness. In all of life's up and down moments, remember Who remained steadfast. Invite the Holy Spirit to prod you in the height of every emotional storm, "Do you do well?" And then lean hard into His grace.

_____
_____
_____
_____
_____
_____

chapter 22

Receipts: The Cross, Our Paid-in-Full Receipt

Monica Schmelter

He himself bore our sins in his body on the tree, that we might die to sin and live to righteousness. By his wounds you have been healed.
(1 Peter 2:24)

A sheriff's deputy showed up at my front door and served me papers. As I scanned through the papers I learned that I was being sued by a collection agency. What? I was being sued for several thousand dollars for a car note that I had paid off in 1996. I needed to find that receipt.

When I couldn't find the receipt in my filing cabinet, I rummaged through my junk drawer like nobody's business. I found receipts for duct tape, Christmas cards, and a microwave that we threw out years ago. No paid-in-full car receipt though. In the midst of worried thoughts about the lawsuit, I took a moment to pray. I asked God for His help in figuring out what I needed to do.

A couple hours later I remembered the name of the finance company and the person I talked to when I made the final payment on the car. Her name was Rebecca. I called her and to my surprise and relief she remembered me. When I told her about the lawsuit and that I needed a paid-in-full receipt she said she would search the system to see what she could find. I prayed silently as she searched. Thankfully, she found the receipt and emailed it to me.

Receipt in Hand

With receipt in hand I called the collection agency and said I had proof of payment. They kept saying this is what our records show. When I said for about the fifth time that I had a receipt they told me to mail them a copy and they would get back with me. When they didn't get back with me I called them again. They told me they would see me in court.

I have a friend who is an attorney so I asked him for advice. He said he would call the collection agency and see what he could do. Later that day he let me know he would represent me in court.

When the court date finally arrived, I was nervous. Before the session started my attorney friend talked with the opposing attorney. Together, they approached the judge. When their talk finally concluded my attorney told me it was resolved as a non-suit. The whole matter was dropped and they had accepted my receipt as proof of payment after all. I created a special place in my file organizer and junk drawer for that particular receipt.

I Wasn't Paying Twice

Even in the midst of my law suit jitters, I felt confident that at some point my receipt would squelch the whole crazy thing. Without that receipt I would have been responsible for paying the debt twice. No way was I going to pay a second time without putting up a fight. Yet that's exactly what we do when we walk around feeling condemned for sins we've already confessed.

Maybe it's the time we repeated a story we promised to keep confidential. Perhaps it's the credit card statement we hid from our husband, or the time we lost our temper while disciplining our children. Whatever it is we've all been there. We've taken a perfectly good day and bogged it down with anxiety and shame about stuff we've already confessed. We take the slate God generously wiped clean with His blood, and re-record our dastardly deeds.

This needless battle can be stopped dead in its tracks with just one truth. That is His Word teaches paid-in-full. His receipt is the once-and-for-all payment for all of our sins. His receipt may not be tucked away in our junk drawer but it's been written with His life and recorded in His Word.

> Belief is the part that requires our effort. God did the hard work by paying the price for our freedom. What we have to do is dare to believe it.

His receipt will clear our hearts and minds in seconds flat when we dare to really believe it.

Dare to Believe It

Belief is the part that requires our effort. God did the hard work by paying the price for our freedom. What we have to do is dare to believe it. This means when a tormenting thought comes our way we have to fight back with His Word. The Bible calls it taking every thought captive to make it obey Christ (2 Corinthians 10:5).

I had the privilege of praying with 83-year-old woman named Irma. I was struck with the sadness in her voice and trembling hands. What was troubling her? Then she finally said it. She was living in guilt over the affair she had when she was 37 years old. When her husband found out he divorced her and was awarded full custody of their children. It took years after the divorce to develop a good relationship with her children.

After I prayed with her she told me that when the affair happened she knew Christ as Savior. It all started when she allowed herself to flirt with a handsome single man in her Sunday school class. What she first regarded as innocent flirting ended up ruining life as she knew it.

As I held her trembling hands she recalled her sinful past. Even though she had repented, attended church, read God's Word, and prayed daily she didn't fully accept Christ's finished work on the cross as full payment for her sins. In Christ, Irma was declared forgiven and blameless.

His Grace is Sufficient

Of course there are situations like Irma's where there are earthly consequences for our sins. But even in those instances the weight of sin is lifted the moment we repent. God's grace is always sufficient, and Jesus finished work on the cross is full payment.

We have to repeatedly discipline our thoughts to obey Christ. Daring to believe His Word means we stop our guilt meltdowns to reflect on what His receipt has provided. We've been declared not guilty. His payment for our sins has already cleared the bank. Scripture says it like this:

> "This includes you who were once far away from God. You were his enemies, separated from him by your evil thoughts and actions. Yet now he has reconciled you to himself through the death of Christ in his physical body. As a result, he has brought you into his own presence,

and you are holy and blameless as you stand before him without a single fault" (Colossians 1:21-22 NLT).

The Bible says God reconciled us to Himself through His death on the cross. Now He brings us into His presence without a single fault. That is some serious goodness right there. I mean that's enough to put a smile of gargantuan proportions on our face and give us exactly what we need to refute those condemning accusations when they come our way. He paid the ultimate price so that we can be forgiven and made clean.

In all likelihood we've all had trouble locating a receipt or two. Perhaps that's why God's Word demonstrates our paid in full receipt in so many passages of Scripture. Let's take a look:

> *Now He brings us into His presence without a single fault. That is some serious goodness right there. I*

"Christ redeemed us from the curse of the law by becoming a curse for us—for it is written, "Cursed is everyone who is hanged on a tree—so that in Christ Jesus the blessing of Abraham might come to the Gentiles, so that we might receive the promised Spirit through faith," (Galatians 3:13-14).

"For our sake he made him to be sin who knew no sin, so that in him we might become the righteousness of God" (2 Corinthians 5:21).

"He himself bore our sins in his body on the tree, that we might die to sin and live to righteousness. By his wounds you have been healed" (1 Peter 2:24).

"In him we have redemption through his blood, the forgiveness of our trespasses, according to the riches of his grace, which he lavished upon us, in all wisdom and insight" (Ephesians 1:7-8).

We Need Reminders

These are just a few examples showing our debt is paid in full as recorded in God's Word. We need these reminders because we live in a fallen world and we have a real enemy who accuses us at every turn. He looks for our weaknesses and launches his attack accordingly.

The enemy of our soul is probably not going to show up at our front door and serve us papers. That would be too obvious. But he does work to remind us of our past and even our present shortcomings and fears. He often works through circumstances and even the words of others to remind us of our faults and transgressions.

When this happens, we need to depend on God's Word as our receipt and proof of payment. We can, with God's help, refuse to pay again and again for something that's already been purchased. We are free from all guilt, sin, and condemnation because of what Jesus Christ did on the cross. The empty tomb is proof of payment. We are whole and free because of the goodness of God expressed through His only Son Jesus Christ. His life is our receipt.

Sorting It Out

List some of your favorite verses that you can rely on as your paid in full receipt (check this chapter for starter ideas).

_____
_____
_____
_____
_____

What can you do to defend yourself when you start feeling condemned or ashamed?

_____

_____

_____

chapter 23

Stray Keys: Locking Up for the Tightest Security

Rhonda Rhea

Make me to know your ways, O LORD; teach
me your paths. Lead me in your truth and
teach me, for you are the God of my salvation;
for you I wait all the day long.
(Psalm 25:4-5)

I hate to even bring this up, but I think my junk drawer had a baby. You always think these kinds of things happen in somebody else's family.

I had *one* junk drawer. That's it. Except now I find that, while I still have that one, it got so overstuffed that its overflow caused it to reproduce itself. Boom. Junk Drawer 2. The frightening sequel. If not legit fright, it at least inspires some anxiety.

The junk drawer offspring is not fully grown. I know this because I can still close it. I have an additional utensil drawer, by the way. It's separate from Junk Drawer 1 or Junk Drawer

2. There are all kinds of cooking utensils in that drawer that I have no idea how to use. Also I don't really cook. But there's a spatula in there that I could probably use if I ever did cook. Except that I can hardly lift it. It's huge. I'm talking, huge. And even though I'll never use it, I will still probably always keep that giant spatula. Mostly because I think it helps me appreciate my drawers that do, in fact, close all the way.

Interestingly, I noticed there are keys in all three drawers. Yes, even the utensil drawer. You know what makes me anxious there? I don't know how it could possibly have happened. Not only do I have no idea how keys got into all three drawers, but I have even less of an idea what any of those keys in any of those three drawers might unlock. There's no small amount of anxiety when I start pondering some locked thing we're all missing out on.

Unlocking the Mysteries

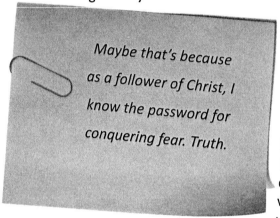

Maybe that's because as a follower of Christ, I know the password for conquering fear. Truth.

While we're exploring the interesting, the mysterious and the anxiety-generating, I realized at the last junk drawer inventory that Junk Drawer 2 has a half dozen slips of paper with assorted passwords on them. OK, let's think this through.

We have passwords to keep various devices and files secure. But all those little scraps of paper are right there in the drawer where anybody can find them. Because we're very conscious of our security issues here. Obviously.

Password anxiety. I'm pretty sure that's also a thing, by the way. You're compelled to choose seven characters, un-guess-able, throw in some capital letters, add the name of a dead pet, sprinkle in a few lower-case letters, include some numeric representation, and, on the whole, the password should eventually grow and evolve into an even better password. Essentially, it should ultimately be able to beat up all the other passwords—make them run crying from the yard.

Anytime I have to choose a new password, my fingers hover over the keys for a solid five minutes. My sweaty fingers. Though I do try to hide any fear. Because I've heard the most evolved passwords can sense it.

It's not that I'm a fearful person. OK, as a child I might've been the only kid whose blanket fort had a panic room. But as an adult, fear isn't such an issue.

Maybe that's because as a follower of Christ, I know the password for conquering fear. Truth. That's it. It doesn't matter what you capitalize or how many numbers you add. Anytime we're afraid, we find strength as we remember what is true, and by faith we hold onto that truth.

Password: T-R-U-T-H

Isaiah 41:10 holds the no-fear message: "'Do not fear [anything], for I am with you; Do not be afraid, for I am your God. I will strengthen you, be assured I will help you; I will certainly take hold of you with My righteous right hand [a hand of justice, of power, of victory, of salvation]'" (AMP).

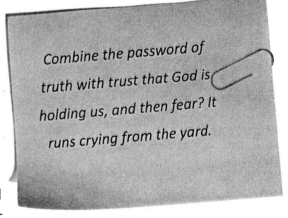

Combine the password of truth with trust that God is holding us, and then fear? It runs crying from the yard.

The Message says it this way, "Don't panic. I'm with you. There's no need to fear for I'm your God. I'll give you strength. I'll help you. I'll hold you steady, keep a firm grip on you."

Nope, no need for a spiritual panic room. We are gripped. The genuine truth is, God gives us the strength for no-fear living as we remember and believe that He holds onto us. Combine the password of truth with trust that God is holding us, and then fear? It runs crying from the yard.

David wrote, "When I am afraid, I put my trust in you. In God, whose word I praise, in God I trust; I shall not be afraid. What can flesh do to me?" (Psalm 56:3-4).

Fear, worry, anxiety. They're emotional responses. Our emotions can be sneaky. It often feels impossible to reason with the rascals. And they're insistent. It's not like we invite fear to take us over. It just does. But our emotions must be taught the truth. By faith, we must believe that despite what our emotions are telling us, the undisputable truth is that we don't need to fear.

> Our emotions can be sneaky. It often feels impossible to reason with the rascals.

God is Bigger Than Your Fear

Think of the things that cause you anxiety. Is there anything you've thought of that's too big for God? Anything that's too hard for Him? Financial stresses? He owns everything. Health issues? He knit your body together. Too much to do? He holds time in His hands. Whatever the source of your stress, the Father loves you, and it's His loving desire to shoulder your burden and squelch your fear. This doesn't mean you do nothing; it means you follow God's direction—and no one else's—on what to do. "Casting all your cares [all your anxieties, all your worries, and all your concerns, once and for all] on Him, for He cares about you [with deepest affection, and watches over you very carefully]" (1 Peter 5:7, AMP).

Our mighty God, the One who lovingly cares for you, is bigger than anything you could ever fear. He is the firewall of all firewalls, as it were, protecting your soul. Wrapping our minds around that truth in faith will delete fear every time. By faith, remember, understand, believe the password: Truth.

Our God has an established record all through His Word of faithfully and lovingly leading His children—in all kinds of brilliant and creative ways. "And the LORD went before them by day in a pillar of cloud to lead them along the way, and by night in a pillar of fire to give them light, that they might travel by day and by night. The pillar of cloud by day and the pillar of fire by night did not depart from before the people" (Exodus 13:21-22). There are firewalls and then there are fire-walls!

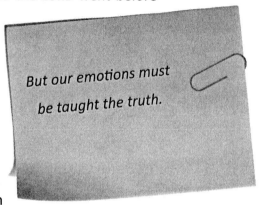

But our emotions must be taught the truth.

It's a Key Truth That Truth Is Key

Whatever is happening around you, let me remind you to remember. Remember, don't forget, be ever-mindful of, the truth about who your great and mighty God is. He is the ultimate problem solver. Understand and embrace that truth. Remembering that password is the key to unlocking the courage to live out your faith victoriously.

As for your other passwords? You might as well also understand that when you finally choose one that's remote enough to be secure, the chances of you remembering it are even more remote than that. Me? I'll just jot mine down. And stuff it in some drawer. And pretend I can close it.

Sorting It Out

Are there fears that have plagued you? Maybe that are plaguing you now? What truth can you list below that can help put those fears in their place? Is there a verse or passage you could write down, and then put to memory—one that could help equip you with fear-conquering truth?

_____

_____

_____

When fear makes it difficult to hang on to the truth, remind yourself to seek the Spirit of truth. He is the Holy Spirit who indwells every believer and will do for us what we can't do on our own. Jesus said, "And I will ask the Father, and he will give you another Helper, to be with you forever, even the Spirit of truth, whom the world cannot receive, because it neither sees him nor knows him. You know him, for he dwells with you and will be in you. 'I will not leave you as orphans; I will come to you'" (John 14:16-18). Write out a prayer asking Him to do in you what you can't do on your own. Ask Him to replace your fear with courage and with His strength.

_____

_____

_____

"And you will know the truth, and the truth
will set you free," (John 8:32).

chapter 24

The Lone Earring: Unmatched

Kaley Rhea

*Iron sharpens iron, and one man
sharpens another.*
(Proverbs 27:17)

It's difficult for me to deal with things that come in pairs. Because when you go through life as I do—quickly and wrestle-y and often without paying enough attention to where you're going—you get to the end of the day and take stock, and you realize you're missing half the pair. Earrings. Gloves. Socks somehow?

And then what do you do?

As previously confessed, I don't tend to get emotionally attached to things. So you'd think I'd just toss the remaining one in the garbage. But I am still an optimist. "I'll probably find the other one. It'll turn up." I probably lost it while traveling halfway across the country. "Eh, I bet it's around here some-where. I'll wait."

So it gets thrown in a drawer. Awaiting the day it will be reunited with its twin. As if the missing one will miraculously

Homeward Bound its way across whatever wilderness lies between it and its mate. If that ever happens, I'll let you know. Keep an eye out on my blog. It'll be a real tear-jerker of an inspirational story.

But so far all my unpaired pairs continue to take up space in a drawer and have no place on my blog. When they lose sight of their buddy, they lose sight of their purpose.

There's No "I" in Lonely—But There Is One in Loneliness So...

Maybe you've felt disconnected that way. Maybe you're going through a season right now where you feel mismatched, misunderstood, mislabeled, misrepresented, mistook, or just plain missing. I've spoken with people in all stages of life who find themselves unexpectedly lonely. Often after a move or a change or an upheaval but sometimes for no discernible reason at all, we can find ourselves feeling a bit set adrift.

> And if I believe God created me mindfully and with purpose and that He's faithful to gift and empower me to fulfill that purpose by his grace, then I have to believe people need me, too.

Or maybe you're more like me. You run on introvert-power, and the idea of chilling in a drawer on your own sounds like your kind of party.

God created me. Knit me together with my introvert tendencies. Built a person who thrives in the quiet places, entertains to the left of the spotlight, creates on the long solo drives. But He did not build me to live totally isolated. When I go too long without connecting with other people, my priorities get mixed up, my sensors turn inward, my compassion for others gets dusty, my wrong thinking goes unchallenged, my joy shrinks like last year's Christmas sweater, my actual immune system doesn't function as well, and the things that promise fulfillment lead to emptiness or discontent. I may not often experience traditional feelings of loneliness when I let my heart deceive me with thoughts of *Alone Is BETTER*. But I honestly start developing symptoms of depression.

Every one of us is designed to live in community, whether introvert or extrovert or a combination of both.

I need people. And if I believe God created me mindfully and with purpose and that He's faithful to gift and empower me to fulfill that purpose by His grace—which I do because that's what He's promises—then I have to believe people need me, too. What a gift! What a special kind of joy and honor.

There's Also an "I" in Community—If that Helps

From the very beginning, from the first person God created, God knew it wasn't good for a human being to be alone. No amount of animal friends would cut it. People need people. It's always been true.

And look at Ecclesiastes 4:9-12 with me. "Two are better than one, because they have a good reward for their toil. For if they fall, one will lift up his fellow. But woe to him who is alone when he falls and has not another to lift him up! Again, if two lie together, they keep warm, but how can ne keep warm alone? And though a man might prevail against one who is alone, two will withstand him—a threefold cord is not quickly broken." This can apply to marriage, but this is not about marriage. It's about person-to-person friendship. This is how we're all to live. Walking with each other. Lifting each other up. Helping each other out. Keeping each other safe.

Now I know, I know, I know people can be difficult. But people can also choose to be easy and lovely and oh so fascinating. People can be disappointing, hurtful, unreliable, inconsiderate, disagreeable, unkind. But people can be enriching, thoughtful, reliable, considerate, companionable, and kind. So we choose the ones to be close with.

I'm certainly not suggesting it's not okay to have some boundaries in place when it comes to interpersonal relationships. By no means would I imply you owe or ought to give your trust to all the humans you meet. You don't, and you oughtn't.

But when we let ourselves be divided, when we let go of fellowship, when we decide isolating ourselves from other believers is easier, we miss out, you guys. We miss out on huge blessings, and we miss out on a huge part of our calling. Remember what Jesus says in John 13:34-35? He tells His bro-postles (that's not a word), "A new commandment I give to you, that you love one another: just as I have loved you, you also are to love one another. By this all people will know that you are my disciples, if you have love for one another."

This is right up at the edge of His time with them, right before He went to the cross. After He'd spent three years living with them and working with them and teaching them and ministering to and through them. They walked together and ate together and annoyed each other and celebrated together. This is one of those things that should still blow our minds, Christ-followers. It would be amazing enough if Jesus only came and died to save us from our sins. That would be incredible. But He went even beyond that. He came and lived here. He showed us how to do relationships with people. He showed how to treat people who loved Him and people who hated Him and people who had no idea what He was talking about. Like "Here you go, little one, let Me show you how we do this." That's nuts. That's love. That's God.

Wordplay Almost Never Proves a Real Point Anyway

I'll be the first to confess, I am incapable of loving consistently. I am incapable of loving like Christ. Except through Christ. There is something brilliant and glorious and miraculous only the Holy Spirit can do in a group of messy humans. Like in Acts 2:42-47, when Christians were new and young and wondering.

It says, "And they devoted themselves to the apostles' teaching and the fellowship, to the breaking of bread and the prayers. And awe came upon every soul, and many wonders and signs were being done through the apostles. And all who believed were together and had all things in common. And they were selling their possessions and belongings and distributing the proceeds to all, as any had need. And day by day, attending the temple together and breaking bread in their homes, they received their food with glad and generous hearts, praising God and having favor with all the people. And the Lord added to their number day by day those who were being saved."

Talk about Messy to Meaningful.

Maybe you're super good at this. If so, I applaud you, and I want to be like you. Maybe you've been trying to connect, to find fellowship, to link arms, and it seems like no one's interested. That can be so frustrating and disheartening! But listen. Don't give up. Continue to be kind. Continue to serve. Continue to pray in the lonely places for God to move mightily, to work in you and through you where you are. He'll do it. He works as powerfully in deserts as he does on mountaintops. He designed you. He knows people need you.

Remember that the believers in Acts 2 later had struggles. So they worked on them.

Maybe you're crafty and you've turned all your unmatched earrings into a fashionable brooch. Brooches are fashionable, right? And you never need a pair of them. They do just fine on their own. Can't I be a brooch, Lord?

Friends, take a lesson from this brooch right here. You need a squad. Even if it's little. Regardless of how tired you may be of the hashtag #squadgoals. Maybe #squadgoals will be over by the time this book comes out. That'd be okay. But the point still stands.

Read Hebrews 10:19-25 with me. "Therefore, brothers, since we have confidence to enter the holy places by the blood of Jesus, by the new and living way that he opened for us through the curtain, that is, through his flesh, and since we have a great priest over the house of God, let us draw near with a true heart in full assurance of faith, with our hearts sprinkled clean from an evil conscience and our bodies washed with pure water. Let us hold fast the confession of our hope without wavering, for he who promised is faithful. And let us consider how to stir up one another to love and good works, not neglecting to meet together, as is the habit of some, but encouraging one another, and all the more as you see the Day drawing near."

Whatever reason you may have for neglecting to meet together, whether it's pain or prejudice or personality or priorities, let's let a part of our worship of the God who made a way for us be loving on the other people He's made. Let's be encouragers of one another. Cheering each other on. Helping each other up. Confident in who we are because of who Jesus is.

That the world would know we are His because we love like He does.

Sorting It Out

When you've battled feelings of loneliness or isolation, what are some ways you step out to connect with people?

_____

_____

_____

Have you faced a hurtful or even devastating circumstance in your past that has caused you to pull inward or that is holding you back from forming healthy bonds with people? That's so real. I just want to encourage you to get loving help for carrying that burden. If you can't bear to talk about it or if you feel you have no one to tell, I want to lovingly, affectionately, with all gentleness remind you that you can share that with Jesus. He knows. Better than anyone, He knows what it is to be hurt.

Start with Him. He is so safe. He can carry all your secrets, all your hurts, all your grief. Speak your thoughts and your fears to Him, and He will hear you even when you don't know where to begin. He is the source of comfort, of strength, of wisdom, of peace.

_____

_____

_____

In the name of community and being considerate, I would like to leave this here:

> "Whoever blesses his neighbor with a loud
> voice, rising early in the morning, will be
> counted as cursing" (Proverbs 27:14).

You can find it on a coffee mug. I checked.

Man, I love the Bible. So relatable. In all seriousness (I guess it doesn't have to be in *all* seriousness), what are some ways you can be a blessing and a friend to someone this week in a way that's good for you both?

One of my favorites is having breakfast. I don't always do well trying to personally interact in the hustle-bustle of pre- and post-church or community activities or whatever—I'm simply not as well-suited for it—but I *love* starting the day connecting one-on-one with a human and some coffee. But you know, I have some night-owl friends who would find my morning-blessings more curse-ish. So we find ways to meet in the middle.

What are some of your favorite how-do-you-do's?

_____

_____

_____

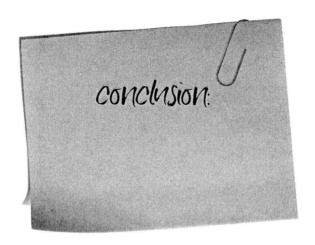

conclusion:

Drawer-Closing Thoughts, Mysteries Revealed

"Closing" thoughts? Yeah, it shouldn't be any real mystery that sometimes these junk drawers of ours simply won't close. From the very beginning of this book, right there in the introduction, we talked about emptying out that drawer, getting rid of the things we don't need. Then all the way through, we've talked about the spiritual junk that can clutter life and the Jesus who can fix every part.

You would think the three of us would have our own physical junk sorted, sifted, and organized, right? After all, we've had an entire book's worth of drawer-sorting input to remind us to do it. Interestingly, each of us can still relate a story or two (possibly 12) about totally unidentifiable items we've found in our respective junk drawers. Mysteries, indeed.

Ordinarily we love a good mystery. A cozy whodunit? Who wouldn't relish that? Maybe the three of us should pool our love for mystery and write one of those books together too.

The Most Beautiful Mystery

Whatever books we write, together or individually, there's one mystery that's ever and always in the center of all we hope to communicate. It's the beautiful mystery of our salvation in and through Jesus Christ alone.

Through the pages of this book, the Lord has used His Word to continue the work of sorting out a lot of our own personal junk. And we'll keep sorting.

It's our ongoing prayer that He has been and will be doing the same for you. In so many areas. Stretching our faith, inspiring us to focus on Him and to seek Him more diligently. In sorting to-do lists and keeping Him at the tip-top of every one of them. In handling worry, insecurity, or fear. Or difficulties, discontentment, or lack of peace. In how we deal with people, how we deal with our material possessions, and how we deal with any out-of-control feelings. Sorting through how we are called and compelled to love, trust, serve, obey, and worship Him. In unpacking and uncluttering much in our faith-walk, according to the Word of God.

As we've touched on those topics and more, each of us has landed unitedly yet uniquely at the cross of Christ. No mystery that we would unite at that most amazing mystery.

Oh the beautiful mystery of our life in Jesus! "For I want you to know how great a struggle I have for you and for those at Laodicea and for all who have not seen me face to face, that their hearts may be encouraged, being knit together in love, to reach all the riches of full assurance of understanding and the knowledge of God's mystery, which is Christ" (Colossians 2:1-2).

Paul struggled with the thought that the new believers in Colossae might swallow some of the lies of false teachers that were springing up. He wanted their hearts to be encouraged with a mystery. Of course, Paul might not have been the best at mystery writing. Because, come on, who introduces the mystery, then solves it in the next word?

The Thrilling Conclusion, in a Word

Then again, who can blame him for rushing to the exciting conclusion? The solution to the glorious mystery—the one-word mystery that encourages hearts, unites in love, leads to riches of understanding—the word is *Christ*. Mystery solved.

And yet at the same time, the mystery continues. It's still mysteriously, miraculously, mind-boggling that the Creator of the universe would provide such a gracious and glorious redemption through the sacrificial death of the Son of God on the cross. Oh, the riches of that "full assurance of understanding." Christ!

The next words in that Colossians passage testify of the mystery of the hidden treasure that is our Savior. "All the treasures of wisdom and knowledge are hidden in Him," (Colossians 2:3 HCSB). The Father has made known to us in Him everything we need to know to have a right relationship with a holy God. Hidden, but now revealed.

You know what this kind of mystery makes us want to do? It makes us want to get to praying, thinking, and going. Praying for boldness and thinking of creative ways to love people by sharing this most glorious mystery reveal, and then get going, getting this marvelous message out in any and every way we can. Paul said, "And *pray* for me, that words may be given to me when I open my mouth, to proclaim boldly the mystery of the good news [of salvation]" (Ephesians 6:19, AMP).

Publicizing—proclaiming—His mystery. We'll keep it up. It's designed to be more of a we-dun-it kind of mystery.

And again, we'll keep the prayers coming for you, that you our reader-friends will be all the more convinced of His power to save and convinced of His ability and willingness to help you through any mess you'll ever encounter. We're praying He will remind you that He will never leave you. His desire is to continue to fill your life to overflowing with marvelous, lasting meaning.

Overflowing. Like our junk drawers (yes, still). But beautiful in every way.

> *Lord, thank You for the astounding, miraculous mystery of Your glorious redemption plan. May we embrace it and live it out every day. And may Your sorting work continue in each of our lives. As You sift through the contents of our*

hearts, souls and minds, show us what to tightly grip, what to let go of, and what to vigilantly kick to the curb. May we walk more purposefully than ever before, all because of Your work in each of us—let us be less weighted down, less hindered...free indeed!

About the Authors

MONICA SCHMELTER

Author, speaker and broadcast jour-nalist, Monica Schmelter, loves a good story. But not just any story. She tells the stories of everyday people. Peo-ple that experience real life, in all its dimension and who journey through struggle to ultimately find the good-ness of God. As a well-endorsed and sought after inspirational speaker, Monica uses the Word to enhance her ability to teach Kingdom principles. She captivates her audi-ences with her ability to simplify the complicated and clarify the unclear. Monica and husband Joseph are parents to Joe who works in IT and regularly fixes all of their devices.

RHONDA RHEA

Rhonda Rhea is a TV personality for Christian Television Network and a humor columnist for great magazines such as *HomeLife, Leading Hearts, The Pathway* and many more. Including the co-authored *Fix Her Upper*, she is the author of 13 books with more un-der contract. Rhonda has been speak-ing at conferences and events from coast to coast for the past couple of decades. She is a pastor's wife, mother of five grown children and says she is now happily beginning a season of harvesting a bumper crop of grand-baby-fruits.

KALEY RHEA

"Making up stories. Telling the truth." Kaley Rhea writes Christian fiction that's heavy on the fun. She and her mom are co-authors of the hilarious Christian romantic comedy, *Turtles in the Road*, with another fiction project under contract and coming soon. When not working on her fiction projects, Kaley writes nonfiction as well and has enjoyed the *Messy to Meaningful* writing and TV journey. With never enough going on, she is also a TV personality for Christian Television Network and other spots across the nation. Kaley lives in the St. Louis area and works at Missouri Baptist University.

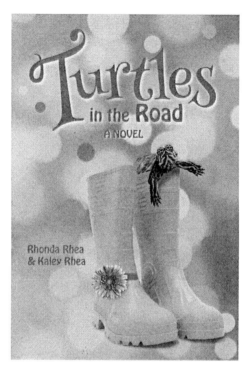

A NOVEL
From

Kaley Rhea
and
Rhonda Rhea

 www.boldvisionbooks.com *195*

From Rhonda Rhea
and
Beth Duewel

HOPE AND LAUGHTER THROUGH A GOD-RENOVATED LIFE

For every woman who could use a life reno—anyone who's ever had heart places that feel a little worn, torn, or tired--we have a God who loves to fix the broken.

  www.boldvisionbooks.com